COASTAL WILDFLOWERS
OF
BRITISH COLUMBIA
AND THE
PACIFIC NORTHWEST

ELIZABETH L. HORN

WHITECAP BOOKS
Vancouver/Toronto

Copyright © 1994 by Elizabeth L. Horn
Whitecap Books Ltd.
Vancouver/Toronto

Published by arrangement with Mountain Press Publishing Co., P.O. Box 2399,
Missoula, Montana 59806

Editing and interior design by Mountain Press Publishing Company
Cover design by Warren Clark
Cover photograph by Michael E. Burch
Interior photographs by Elizabeth L. Horn

Canadian Cataloguing in Publication Data

Horn, Elizabeth L.
    Coastal wildflowers of British Columbia and the Pacific Northwest

    Includes bibliographical references and index.
    ISBN 1-55110-166-1

    1. Wild flowers—British Columbia—Identification. 2. Wild flowers—
Northwest Coast of North America—Identification. 3. Coastal flora—
Northwest Coast of North America—Identification. I. Title
QK203.B7H67 1994   582.13'09711   C93-091930-0

Printed in Hong Kong

This book is dedicated to Francis Horn,
who shared his Oregon heritage with me,
and to Frances Horn,
the granddaughter he never knew.

Contents

Acknowledgments   vii

Preface   1

Pacific Coast Map   2

How to Use This Book   7

Beaches and Dunes   9

Wetlands   33

Cliffs and Grasslands   67

Brushfields   113

Coastal Forests   143

Wildflower Photography   164

Plant Illustrations
    Flower Parts   166
    Primary Inflorescence Types   166
    Leaf Shapes   167
    Leaf Arrangements   168
    Leaf Structure   168
    Coastal Forest Conifers   169

Glossary   170

Selected References   173

Index   174

Acknowledgments

This little book was first published in 1980. It was not done in a vacuum—many friends and colleagues offered help and encouragement along the way. Their help made it a very enjoyable project.

I recall the special help I received for the first edition from Dr. Kenton Chambers, Oregon State University, and from Dr. John Sawyer, Humboldt State University, who assisted with plant identification and photographic locations and allowed me to use the university herbarium facilities. Dr. Sawyer also helped in reviewing the original manuscript and made many suggestions that aided its readability.

During the intervening years, I have made many additional visits to the coast of the Pacific Northwest. The wildflowers of Cascade Head and Cape Perpetua seem timeless, always greeting me upon my return visits. There have been additional opportunities to visit the coastal forests of Vancouver Island, Redwoods National Park, Prairie Creek Redwoods State Park, and Patrick's Point to find shade-loving wildflowers. The windswept beaches of Olympic National Park, Long Beach (Washington), Oregon Dunes National Recreation Area, and Point Reyes National Seashore were only a few of the scenic shorelines that gave me the opportunity to photograph new species. The headlands of Cape Blanco and the Mendocino coastline mixed the wildflowers of open grassland, beach, and brushy slopes. Numerous unnamed waysides, glens, and beaches between these points provided myriad delightful wildflower haunts.

Many friends have asked whether this book would ever be printed again. I am very thankful once again for the assistance of Dr. John Sawyer, who reviewed the manuscript and nomenclature changes, and for the help of Veva Stansell, Gold Beach Ranger Station, Siskiyou National Forest, in finding photographic locations. I appreciate the fine work and support of the staff at Mountain Press for putting together this new edition, for being willing to add numerous photographs, and for doing an overall professional job. This book is a much more complete guide to coastal wildflowers than the first.

Preface

Windswept bluffs, damp salt spray, open expanses of golden sand, vistas of rugged vertical cliffs, against a background of deep blue ocean or fog-shrouded sea—the Pacific Northwest coast possesses all of these and has an attraction all its own. Integral to these scenes are wildflowers and flowering shrubs, which add both color and appeal.

This book was designed to help you identify the most conspicuous wildflowers and flowering shrubs you may encounter as you travel along the Pacific shore from British Columbia through the northern part of California. More than 150 species are included here, accompanied by full-color photographs. In addition to the common and scientific name for each plant, I've tried to include information on its range, the kinds of places it is found, and its historical uses. This information always makes a plant more interesting and easier to remember. The flowering times and sizes of many species are also noted; however, these should only be considered a general guide. Many of the plants range the full length of the Pacific coast, meaning that they will bloom earlier along the California shore than they will along the British Columbia coast. Variations in soil and topography also influence the blooming time, as well as the size a plant may grow. The common yarrow, for instance, may grow only a few inches tall on a sandy dune where drying winds blow constantly; on the northern slope of a coastal headland, protected from the wind and firmly rooted in deeper soil, the same species may grow nearly two feet tall!

Take this little book with you when you visit the coast. Use it as an introduction to the many wildflowers you will see. Take the time to learn a little about each as you go. Take note of the type of area where each plant grows and consider it a re-found friend when you next encounter it. You'll discover that knowing a little about the plants you come across will add a lot of fun to your trip and make it far more interesting.

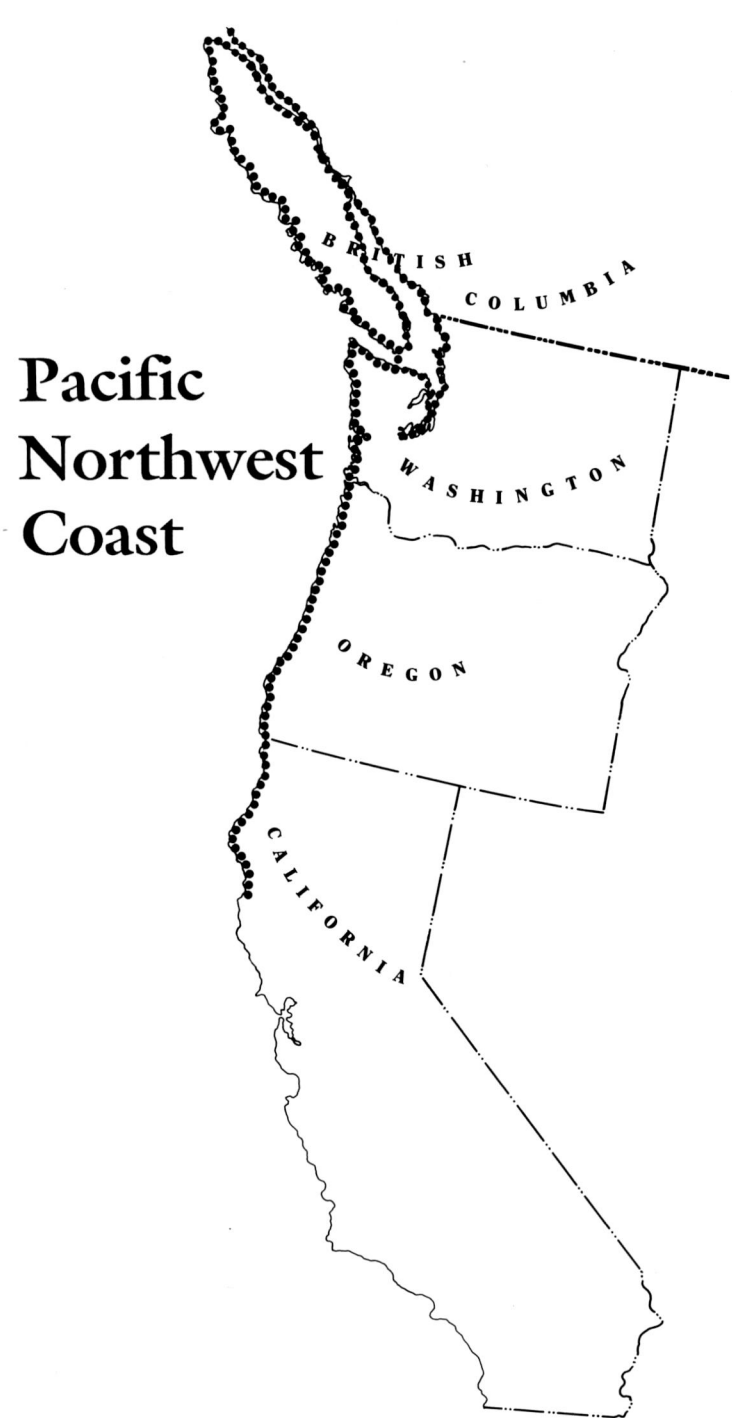

Pacific Northwest Coast

BRITISH COLUMBIA

WASHINGTON

OREGON

CALIFORNIA

The Coastal Scene

Rugged headlands, small sandy coves, and broad plains that may be partially hilled with sand dunes or covered by dense forest blend to produce unmatched beauty and scenic variety. The mild coastal climate allows visitation year-round and also contributes to the long flowering season. Several interesting shrubs, such as the chaparral broom and silk tassel, bloom during the winter months. Springtime begins in February and sandy spits and plains may still be covered with blossoms in August, especially along the coasts of northern Oregon, Washington, and British Columbia. It is possible to follow spring northward, as some widespread species bloom in March along the California coast but do not bloom until later in the spring or early summer farther north.

Our Pacific Northwest coast is blessed with a moderate year-round climate. The constant temperature of the vast Pacific Ocean is largely responsible for this. In addition, northwesterly winds dominate during the summer months (bringing cool air), while southwesterly winds dominate during the winter months (bringing warm air). The result is cool summers and mild winters. Coastal beaches may be bathed in fog during the summer when the cooler breezes off the ocean meet a warm inland air mass. Precipitation is quite high, especially in the northern part of the coastal range, and occurs mostly in the winter. In summer, moisture is retained due to low temperatures and the presence of coastal fog.

Coastal Vegetation

Climate largely determines the type of vegetation that grows in an area, but other factors, such as topography and underlying soils, are important. Plants that grow together in an association under the same general conditions are called plant communities. The collective surroundings of any plant is called its habitat.

The coastal climate makes a transition from temperate to Mediterranean as you travel south. Vegetation along the British Columbia and Washington coasts is typified by dense forests and undergrowth, but a shift takes place in Oregon, and the southern Oregon coast begins displaying more California plant species. Summers here are warmer and drier than farther north. Open slopes are more common, with ravines and stream banks providing the only habitat for plants requiring more moisture.

The wildflowers and flowering shrubs described in this book are grouped according to the habitats in which they are most typically found. Rarely, however, are the lines between these areas completely sharp. Often one area blends into another, forming what is called an ecotone. For example, where brush has begun to invade an open grassland, salmonberry

might grow on the edges of the grassland and be a dominant plant in the resulting brushfield. The tiger lily grows well on exposed, grassy headlands, but also thrives in the scattered shade at the edge of a brush thicket or along a partially shaded roadway through the redwood forest. Sometimes, conditions may allow a versatile plant to grow successfully in more than one area. Salal, for example, dominates brushy areas along coastal bluffs and forms an impenetrable hedge. It also grows as the understory of a shady, coastal forest. Sometimes moisture conditions change as the summer progresses. For example, ladies' tresses, a small orchid, is frequently found in the moist swales known as deflation plains on the leeside of a sand dune. However, by the time it blooms in late July, the sandy substrate in which it is embedded may appear quite dry. This seasonal change is important on many coastal headlands, where a thin layer of soil over the basalt substrate supports a grassy community. Moisture is plentiful in this thin layer of soil during the spring, making it a good place to look for early blooming wildflowers. By midsummer, the soil is dry and only golden and brown grasses remain.

Nonetheless, most plants typically grow together as a community within a specific type of habitat. You will soon learn that where you find sand verbena, searocket will not be far away. Small creeping buttercup will usually be found not far from golden-eyed grass and tinker's penny. Plants in this book are grouped in five habitats: open beaches and dunes, wetlands, cliffs and grasslands, brushfields, and coastal forests. A brief description precedes each section.

5

How to Use This Book

As you explore the beaches of the Pacific coast and hike the trails to grassy headlands, you'll see a rich variety of wildflowers and flowering shrubs. The book is simple to use out in the field. Match the photo and word description with your plant. The plants shown in this book are arranged by the habitat in which they are most often found: beaches and dunes, wetlands, cliffs and grasslands, brushfields, and coastal forests. Look around you and decide which habitat section in the book is likely to contain your plant. Within each habitat, plant families are listed alphabetically by common name. Individual plant species in a family are listed alphabetically by scientific name. To help you recognize members of the same plant family, a general description of those families well-represented along the Pacific coast precedes the section containing the most examples of that particular family. When members of a plant family are found in more than one habitat, I have noted the pages where you will find their descriptions.

Information about each plant has been kept straightforward, with botanical terminology kept to a minimum. (If you do see a term you do not understand, however, check the glossary and illustrations in the back of the book.) Each plant heading includes the family, the common name, and the scientific name of the plant described. The scientific names generally follow those listed in Hitchcock and Cronquist's *Flora of the Pacific Northwest* (Seattle: University of Washington Press, 1973) or *The Jepson Manual: Higher Plants of California* (Edited by James C. Hickman. Berkeley, Los Angeles, London: University of California Press, 1993).

7

Beaches and Dunes

Few plants survive in any kind of numbers on the open sand. The constantly shifting sand makes it hard for them to obtain sufficient footing. As a result, most plants that live on the beach have deep taproots and stout stems that can adapt to being alternately buried or exposed by the blowing sand. Beach silvertop thrives partly because it has a deep taproot. The sheathing petioles, or leaf stalks, are alternately buried or exposed by the sand. Other plants, such as the sand verbena and beach morning glory, have broad, succulent leaves that help trap the sand and keep it in place.

Most of the plants growing on open sand reproduce vegetatively instead of by seed. This means that new plants are formed by shoots, suckers, underground stems, cuttings, or by similar means. Plants relying on seeds are at a disadvantage in sand. Seeds may be buried too deep or left exposed to dry in the salt air and wind. The seeds of the gray beach pea and beach silvertop are exceptions. These seeds are larger and heavier than sand grains, allowing them to be buried beneath the sand where they will not dry out. Their mass and weight gives them some stability during the critical germination period. Coast strawberry and Pacific silverweed spread by stolons, or runners, much like the garden strawberry does. Horizontal stems spread over the surface and roots form at the nodes, resulting in a new plant.

BUCKWHEAT FAMILY

Polygonaceae

Coast Buckwheat

Eriogonum latifolium

Coast buckwheat decorates sandy swales and beaches. It is also found on sea bluffs and rocks, where it thrives in the full force of coastal storms. A dense tuft of woolly leaves grows from a woody stem and forms the base of the plant, with the leafless, flowering stems extending 12 to 14 inches above it. The clusters of flowers are pink or white—or shades in between. Several varieties occur along the Pacific coast, but those types are not dealt with here. Coast buckwheat blooms from May through October.

Found from central California to southwestern Oregon.

Beach Knotweed

Polygonum paronychia

Beach knotweed is a sprawling, woody plant with pale pink flowers tucked in clusters of leaves at the tips of the branches. These leaves are about an inch long, elliptic in shape, and rolled under along the edge, a feature that helps conserve moisture in the windy, coastal climate. Beach knotweed is known as a "pioneer" plant because it is one of the first plants able to take root and grow in dunes and other sandy places, helping stabilize the substrate so that other plants may eventually take hold.

Found from Vancouver Island to Monterey, California.

CARPETWEED FAMILY

Aizoaceae

Sea Fig

Carpobrotus chilensis

The sea fig forms extensive mats that spread out over sandy flats and dunes or coastal bluffs. The thick, fleshy leaves are opposite each other on the stem and resemble three-sided pencils. They are often tinged with purple. The magenta or purple flowers are at the ends of the stems.

Found from Chile to southern Oregon.

Similar plant: The **hottentot fig** (*Carpobrotus edule*) is also a prostrate, spreading plant; however, its flowers are yellow, fading to pink as they age, and its leaves are brighter green. It is a native of Africa and has been planted extensively along roadways to stabilize the banks and prevent erosion.

Coast Buckwheat
Eriogonum latifolium

Beach Knotweed
Polygonum paronychia

Sea Fig   *Carpobrotus chilensis*

Hottentot Fig   *Carpobrotus edulis*

11

EVENING PRIMROSE FAMILY   Onagraceae

Other members of the evening primrose family are described on pages 72 and 116.

Beach Primrose   *Camissonia cheiranthifolia*

This fleshy-leaved, prostrate plant can be found on beaches and dunes. Its stout stems stretch across the surface of the sand, radiating from a leafy rosette. The thick leaves have a slightly gray color. The four-petaled flowers are about an inch across. They are bright yellow when they first open, but may turn pink or red with age. This evening primrose is barely a few inches tall, although the sprawling stems may be a foot or more long.

Found from British Columbia south through California.

Farewell-to-spring   *Clarkia amoena*

Farewell-to-spring delineates the edge of beaches and low shoreline bluffs with colorful lavender flowers at the begining of the summer. It is usually within the range of salt spray. The flowers are four-petaled and cup-shaped, with each inch-long petal marked with a centrally located splotch of red color. The stems may grow nearly 2 feet tall; near shore, they may be much shorter. The weak stems either sprawl in the golden grasses or stand upright. The name farewell-to-spring indicates the change of season from spring to summer along the coast.

Found from northern California to southwestern Oregon.

Evening Primrose   *Oenothera hookeri*

These stout plants grow 2 to 3 feet tall on sandy beaches and waysides along the coast. Often, the stems and leaves are tinged with red, as are the unopened floral buds. A biennial (meaning the plant sprouts and over-winters before blooming the following year), this evening primrose may be considered weedy. Nevertheless, when the full, golden, four-petaled blossoms are open, it is a beauty. Opening in late afternoon and remaining open through the night, the flowers are several inches across. Good places to look for it include the beaches south of Orick and at Lagoon State Park.

Found through much of the western states.

Beach Primrose
Camissonia cheiranthifolia

Farewell-to-spring   *Clarkia amoena*

Evening Primrose   *Oenothera hookeri*

Evening Primrose   *Oenothera hookeri*

13

FOUR O'CLOCK FAMILY   Nyctaginaceae

SAND VERBENA   *Abronia* **species**
Sand verbena, like the rest of the four o'clock family, is characterized by tubular flowers tucked into dense, circular heads. Sand verbena makes a bright, colorful spot on the sandy landscape of open dunes. It has stout, deep taproots and sprawling, branching stems that seem to hold both the sand and the plant in place. Glandular leaves are often encased with grains of sand. It is speculated by some that the weight of these accumulated sand grains may even help hold the plant in place! Although the individual flowers are small, they occur in ball-shaped clusters that are several inches in diameter and, therefore, quite conspicuous. Sand verbena reproduces successfully by seed as well as vegetatively.

Two species of sand verbena occur along the Pacific coast.

Yellow Sand Verbena   *Abronia latifolia*
The tubular flowers of this sand verbena are yellow, each tube being about a half inch long. Each flower cluster is rounded and on its own stem. Yellow sand verbena is a prostrate plant, sprawling over the open sand, forming hummocks that resemble small bushes from a distance.

Many coastal Indian tribes dug the large roots of sand verbena and used them for food. Both the Klallam and Makah of Washington State ate these roots.

Found from Vancouver Island through California.

Pink Sand Verbena   *Abronia umbellata*
The pink sand verbena is very similar to the yellow sand verbena and is more common along the southern portion of the Pacific coast, where it inhabits coastal beaches and dunes. The flowers are slightly smaller and are pink or purple. It may be found alongside yellow sand verbena on northern California beaches such as those at the mouth of the Mad River.

Found from Oregon to Baja California.

Yellow Sand Verbena *Abronia latifolia*

Pink Sand Verbena *Abronia umbellata*

MORNING GLORY FAMILY Convolvulaceae

Beach Morning Glory *Calystegia soldanella*

Trailing its 2-foot-long stems across the sandy beaches and open dunes, beach morning glory is recognized by its 2-inch-long, fleshy, kidney-shaped leaves and trumpet-shaped pink or white flowers. The flowers bloom throughout the summer, but sometimes fail to open on a cloudy day. This morning glory helps bind the sand and seems to flourish where sand has not been stabilized. Many of the morning glories of the Northwest are actually native to other parts of the world and were introduced here. Beach morning glory is an exception and is native to the dunes of the Pacific coast.

Found from British Columbia to southern California.

MUSTARD FAMILY Cruciferae

Members of the mustard family found on cliffs and grasslands are described on page 86.

Searocket *Cakile maritima*

Sprouting on open sand, this little annual has fleshy leaves and stems. Some of searocket's stems are upright, branching freely from the base, while others spread across the sand. The alternate leaves are about an inch long and are pinnately lobed. Pale purple flowers are clustered near the ends of the stems. Fairly common on Pacific beaches, searocket blooms through most of the summer.

Found from British Columbia to California.

Similar plant: Another **searocket** (*Cakile edentula*) also occurs along the Pacific coast and looks very similar; however, the succulent leaves of this searocket are merely lobed or wavy-edged, not divided.

PARSLEY FAMILY Umbelliferae

Other members of the parsley family are described on pages 54 and 88 to 92.

Beach Silvertop *Glehnia littoralis*

Beach silvertop forms compact little clumps on beaches and dune areas, especially where sand has not yet become stabilized. A prostrate plant, it is characterized by compound, leathery leaves that are quite woolly on the lower surface; tight, round clusters of tiny white flowers; and balls of corky-winged fruit. Because it thrives in areas of drifting sand, beach silvertop quite often appears stemless, with even the sheathing of leaf stems partially buried in the sand. In actuality, it is deeply rooted in the unstable sand by a stout taproot. The lower stem and leaves can withstand alternate burying and exposure because they have adapted to the changing sand levels.

The flowers begin to bloom during the early part of the summer, and plants often bear flowers until the end of the season. It is possible to find both flowers and fruit on the same plant in August!

Found along the coast from Alaska through northern California.

Beach Morning Glory *Calystegia soldanella*

Searocket *Cakile maritima*

Beach Silvertop *Glehnia littoralis*

17

PEA FAMILY   Leguminosae

The pea family is an extremely important group of plants, usually characterized by showy flowers and compound leaves. The flowers resemble those of the garden pea and have five petals. These are arranged with two lateral petals called wings, an upper petal that is usually enlarged and called a banner, and two lower petals that form a keel and are sometimes fused together. The stamens are tucked within the keel. The fruit is called a legume and is a pod. Many members of this family are grown commercially, including the bean, pea, clover, alfalfa, soybean, and sweet pea.

Other members of the pea family are described on pages 54 and 130.

SWEET PEA   *Lathyrus* species

The genus *Lathyrus* is distinguished by one-sided racemes of flowers (resembling those of the garden sweet pea) and pinnately compound leaves, which usually have tendrils (a slender piece of stem or leaf that coils around other plants or objects for support).

Beach Pea   *Lathyrus japonicus*

Found on sandy beaches and tangled amid the grasses of the foredune, beach pea has inch-long, purple or rose flowers and dark green, pinnately compound leaves. The trailing stems grow up to 3 feet long. Beach pea spreads by rhizomes, or creeping underground stems, that hold the plant securely in the loose sand. New shoots sprout from this underground stem, forming a new plant.

Found along the coast from Alaska to northern California.

Silky Beach Pea   *Lathyrus littoralis*

Gray beach pea may be found on foredunes and partially stabilized dunes, where its prostrate, sprawling stems are partially hidden by the more upright stems of the beach grass. The leaves have a silky appearance due to a covering of soft hairs. The flowers grade in color from white to pink or purple. Although the genus *Lathyrus* has tendrils at the tips of its pinnately compound leaves, in this species the tendrils have been replaced by small green appendages.

Another name for this plant is Chinook licorice, referring to the use of this plant by some Indians who roasted and ate the root.

Found from Washington to central California.

Beach Pea *Lathyrus japonicus*   **Silky Beach Pea** *Lathyrus littoralis*

Silky Beach Pea *Lathyrus littoralis*

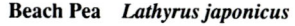

LUPINE
Lupinus species

Lupines are showy members of the pea family. They have pea-shaped flowers that are borne in a raceme, a cluster of flowers, each with its own stalk, arranged along a central stem with the lower lateral flowers blooming before the ones at the tip. Lupines are usually identified by their palmately compound leaves—the leaflets spread from a common point, like the fingers of a hand. Although many individual lupines are difficult to distinguish from each other, the group as a whole is easy to recognize.

Bush Lupine
Lupinus arboreus

Bush lupine colors dunes and other sandy spots during the early summer with its golden plumes of flowers. A woody shrub, 3 to 5 feet tall, it lines coastal roadways and bays. Like other lupines, it has palmately compound leaves and clusters of pea-shaped flowers. *Arboreus* means "treelike"; however, the branching main trunk makes this plant quite bushy. Growing readily from seed, it flowers after the second or third year and is a very attractive shrub.

Native only to the central California coast, it has been widely planted for dune stabilization and has also been introduced into other parts of the world for this purpose.

Found along the Pacific coast from central California to Vancouver Island.

Seashore Lupine
Lupinus littoralis

A long, thick taproot holds seaside lupine in place so well that sand often blows out from around the plant, leaving a low mound, or hummock. Some plants resemble a small, sprawling shrub 1 or 2 feet high, while other seaside lupine stems are prostrate, stretching over the sand. The flowers are pale blue. You'll find this lupine in a variety of places, from open dunes to sandy bluffs, but it is never far from shore.

Found from British Columbia to northern California.

Giant Vetch
Vicia gigantea

You'll find giant vetch spreading and crawling over piles of driftwood debris at the edge of the beach. The stout, climbing stems are 3 to 6 feet long and have pinnately compound leaves of sixteen to thirty leaflets. A fine, slender tendril aids giant vetch's spread by coiling around other plants or pieces of driftwood. The flowers are reddish-purple or bronze and about an inch long. They are borne in linear clusters.

Found along the Pacific coast from Alaska to northern California.

Bush Lupine *Lupinus arboreus*

Bush Lupine *Lupinus arboreus*

Seashore Lupine *Lupinus littoralis*

Giant Vetch *Vicia gigantea*

21

PINK FAMILY
Caryophyllaceae

A member of the pink family found on bluffs and grasslands is described on page 94.

Sea Purslane
Honkenya peploides

Also known as seabeach sandwort, sea purslane is not noted for its flowers, which are very tiny, barely a quarter inch across. They are nearly hidden, tucked between the fleshy, inch-long leaves, which appear to wrap around them. This is significant because the species name is derived from the ancient Greek word *peplis*, meaning "cloak." This plant forms distinctive mounds on many coastal beaches, its somewhat trailing stems sprawling across the beach and cobblestones.

Very few plants are able to tolerate the open beach. Since most seeds are capable of germinating in wet sand, large numbers of seedlings can often be found on the beach in the spring. Nevertheless, most of them succumb quickly to the elements. Some plants do not have the ability to develop an extensive root system quickly to reach deeper water levels as the sand dries. Constant coastal winds may buffet the plant unmercifully before it can establish itself. Salt spray, carried inland by these winds, may deposit drying salt particles on the plant's surface. Blowing sand may alternately bury and expose the plant's roots and stem. The hardy, bushlike shape and thick cuticle on the leaves and stems contribute to sea purslane's ability to survive on the coastal beach.

Found from Alaska to Oregon. Sea purslane is a circumpolar species.

PLANTAIN FAMILY
Plantaginaceae

Seaside Plantain
Plantago maritima

This simple little plant has a rosette of basal, linear leaves that are somewhat leathery to touch. The green, four-petaled flowers are borne in a dense spike growing up to 5 inches tall. Seaside plantain can be found along the edges of beaches, usually along the rocky edges or on the bluffs above. It blooms throughout most of the summer.

Found from Alaska to southern California.

Sea Purslane   *Honkenya peploides*

Seaside Plantain   *Plantago maritima*

ROSE FAMILY
Rosaceae

Members of the rose family found in wetlands are described on page 58, one found on cliffs and grasslands is described on page 98, and those growing in brushy areas are described on pages 132 to 138.

Beach Strawberry
Fragaria chiloensis

Creeping over sandy bluffs and dry plains, coast strawberry has large white, five-petaled flowers nearly an inch in diameter and glossy-green, three-parted leaves. As with all strawberry plants, it spreads readily by stolons—horizontal stems that grow over the surface of the ground and root to start a new plant. Where coast strawberry is abundant, it speckles the ground with its white blossoms. The strawberries that appear later in the summer are much smaller than the flowers. Careful searching among the leaves on sandy flats and bluffs should find these tasty, if gritty, morsels. You will have to be early, though, because small rodents and many species of birds relish these fruits.

Because the shiny leaves and large white flowers are so attractive, coast strawberry is often planted in coastal gardens for ground cover. Small rooted cuttings do best in sandy, well-drained soil. If placed about 18 inches apart, their stolons will fill in an area after one growing season. The spot will be particularly attractive if pieces of driftwood are incorporated.

Found along the coast from Alaska to California and also along the coasts of South America and Hawaii.

Pacific Silverweed
Potentilla anserina

Pacific silverweed is never far from the shore, preferring sandy bluffs, damp swales between dunes, and wet coastal marshes. Like the strawberry, silverweed spreads readily by stolons, or runners. Instead of a white flower, however, the silverweed blossom is bright yellow and is, therefore, sometimes mistaken for a buttercup. An inch or more across, it is a conspicuous flower. The leaves are pinnately compound, meaning the leaflets are spread linearly along a centerline, like the parts of a feather.

Pacific silverweed roots were eaten by several coastal Indian tribes, who prepared them by steaming and dipping them in whale oil before eating.

Found in damp areas along the coast from Alaska to southern California.

Beach Strawberry   **Beach Strawberry**
Fragaria chiloensis   *Fragaria chiloensis*

Pacific Silverweed   *Potentilla anserina*

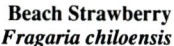

SUNFLOWER FAMILY   Compositae

Other members of the sunflower family are described on pages 62, 102 to 110, 140, and 158.

Beach Silverweed   *Ambrosia chamissonis*

Also known as silver bursage or beach burr, beach silverweed almost escapes notice because its flowers are not particularly conspicuous or colorful. The large mats of silvery green leaves, however, catch one's eye. They form little hummocks on open beaches and dunes. The prostrate stems grow from a large taproot and are between 2 and 4 feet long. Short white hairs cover the thick, spatulate leaves, giving them a silvery appearance. The tassel of flowers at the tips of the branches produce the pollen, while the seed-producing flowers are usually found in the leaf axils along the length of the stem or tucked at the base of the pollen-bearing cluster of flowers. Beach silverweed blooms in July. The fruits are prickle-covered burrs and appear in August and September.

Found from Vancouver Island south along the coast through California.

Beach Sagewort   *Artemisia pycnocephala*

Resembling sagebrush, to which it is closely related, beach sagewort draws attention because of its attractive, silvery foliage. The stout, simple stems emerge from a woody base and have leaves that are finely dissected and covered with white, woolly hairs. The flowering stems carry small, dense, yellow flower heads arranged at the end of the stems. The plants themselves resemble small shrubs and hug the dunes where they grow. An individual plant grows about a foot tall.

Found from central California to southwestern Oregon.

Beach Aster   *Corethrogyne californica*

This little plant is very attractive. It has gray-green leaves that are spatulate-shaped, with the broadest part pointing away from the stem. The stems extend 12 inches or more, sprawling across the sand on partially stabilized dunes at the edge of the beach. In the middle of summer the tips of the leafy stems bend upward, unfolding into an asterlike floral head with lilac or purple ray flowers. Where several plants occur together, the sprawling, creeping leaves form a loosely woven mat, with the colorful flowers extending 4 to 6 inches above them. Look carefully for beach aster amid the tufts of beach grass.

Found from central California north into southern Oregon.

Beach Silverweed
Ambrosia chamissonis

Beach Sagewort
Artemisia pycnocephala

Beach Aster   *Corethrogyne californica*

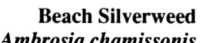

Beach Gumweed   *Grindelia stricta*

Prostrate mats of this yellow-flowered plant inhabit sandy flats and seaside bluffs. The sessile leaves are smooth, somewhat leathery, and inclined to sprawl, although they may reach upward 6 to 12 inches from the ground. The flower heads are quite showy; it is the unfolded buds, however, that are distinctive. They exude a milky white substance. The flowers bloom from June through September. Look for this plant when you visit the beaches and bluffs along State Highway 1 in northern California.

Found from central California to southern Oregon. Another gumweed is described on page 62.

Cat's Ear   *Hypochaeris radicata*

Easily mistaken for the common dandelion (*Taraxacum officinale*), cat's ear decorates deflation plains and disturbed sandy places with its abundance of yellow flowers. All the leaves, which are irregularly toothed along the edges, are basal and covered with stiff, short hairs. The flowering stems are 6 to 24 inches tall and usually branch to bear more than one flowering head.

Found throughout much of the Pacific Northwest.

Similar plant: **Hawkbit** (*Leontodon nudicaulis*) also has basal leaves and dandelionlike flowerheads. The leaves, however, form a dense rosette that is flattened against the ground. The flowering stems are unbranched, each bearing a single flower head. It is a much smaller plant, rarely exceeding 6 inches.

All three of these plants (cat's ear, hawkbit, and dandelion) are native to Europe and are generally considered weeds. Indeed, they invade lawns, pastures, and gardens, where they can be serious pests. Amid the dune grasses, however, they have become naturalized and add a bit of color.

Dune Goldenrod   *Solidago spathulata*

Also called sticky goldenrod, this plant thrives in dune areas that have become partially stabilized with grassy vegetation. It grows up to 2 feet tall and has spatulate-shaped leaves, as its species name implies. The best way to recognize it, though, is by its sticky and aromatic leaves, which look as though they have been recently varnished. This goldenrod colors ocean dunes and swales in late summer and early fall. Good places to look for it include the Clatsop Spit at the mouth of the Columbia and the dunes near Humboldt Bay in northern California.

Found from central California to British Columbia.

Beach Gumweed *Grindelia stricta*

Cat's Ear *Hypochaeris radicata*

Dune Goldenrod *Solidago spathulata*

Seaside Tansy   *Tanacetum camporatum*

Also called western tansy, this stout-stemmed plant grows in open dunes and sandy flats, sometimes forming hummocks. The leaves are finely divided, almost fernlike, and have fine, white hairs. The half-inch-wide flower heads lack ray flowers and resemble pale yellow buttons. These are very numerous and are located at the end of the stems. Where tansy has formed hummocks on the sand, it looks like a yellow-flowered bush.

Found along the coast from British Columbia through northern California.

WATERLEAF FAMILY   Hydrophyllaceae

Silvery Phacelia   *Phacelia argentea*

Silvery phacelia is well named. The stiff, white hairs covering the leaves produce a silvery effect in the sunlight. A stout perennial plant, this phacelia has round or oval leaves and dense clusters of white or pale yellow flowers. These flowers are in round scorpioid heads, meaning the flowers are along a coiled or curved stem. Silvery phacelia grows 4 to 12 inches tall and blooms during the early summer, although a few blossoms may be found through August. Look for it in sandy waysides as you travel the Pacific coast.

Found from southern Oregon to northern California.

Seaside Tansy   *Tanacetum camphoratum*

Silvery Phacelia   *Phacelia argentea*

Wetlands

Wetlands can be either saltwater or freshwater. Poor drainage on the flat coastal plain results in many swales and moist roadside ditches. The coast is also dotted with many lakes and marshes. Typical lowland plants in these areas include the cattail, skunk cabbage, spirea, and pond lily.

A wetland unique to the coast is the deflation plain, where the wind has carried the sand away, stripping the surface down to the water table. Deflation plains normally occur on the lee side of the foredune, which immediately parallels the shore, or at the base of a large, moving dune system. Often, deflation plains are completely covered with water during the winter months, making them important stopping places for migrating waterfowl. Many birds that spend the summer breeding season in Alaska and northern Canada winter in these wet, coastal areas. By early summer, much of the water is gone and the area is merely damp, providing perfect conditions for a wide variety of small wildflowers. Some plants of the open beach also occur here. Wetlands are rich in plant diversity and support both herbaceous plants and many kinds of flowering shrubs. Small creeping buttercup shares deflation plains with labrador tea, sundew, tinker's penny, gentian, and monkeyflower, to name but a few. By late August, however, the water table has usually dropped so far that only dry sand, rushes, sedges, and leafy shrubs are easily seen.

A special type of wetland is the coastal seep, or bog, that forms between coastal dunes, or in other places where poor drainage exists. Here, insectivorous plants, such as the cobra lily and the sundew, are found. They are usually associated with other colorful plants, such as labrador tea and bog laurel.

Unique to the shoreline are saltwater wetlands, where the tide may periodically cover mudflats and bays or fill the mouths of sea-going streams and alternately leave these same areas exposed. The flush of sea water brings with it the tiny plant and animal life that makes saltwater wetlands so rich. Plants that live on these shores must adapt to the alternating tides. For part of each day they are bathed in salt water and must have strong root systems to hold them in place against the surging stream of the ocean. They must also have a tough surface on their stems and leaves to withstand the penetrating salt of sea water. It is here that you might look for the colorful jaumea and dainty sea milkwort.

Coastal wetlands, once thought to be wastelands, and often drained to make way for other uses, are now being recognized for the valuable habitat they provide.

ARUM FAMILY Araceae

Skunk Cabbage *Lysichitum americanum*

One of the first signs of spring along the coast is the appearance of the yellow hoods of skunk cabbage. They fill swales and waterways and even occur in otherwise well-groomed pastures. Although skunk cabbage also occurs inland, it is most conspicuous along the Pacific coast strip. The brightly colored hood (botanically known as a *spathe*) encloses the skunk cabbage flowers, which are clustered at the upper end of a 1-foot-tall stalk. The floral stalk eventually outgrows the protective yellow hood, and by mid- or late summer, large, green cabbagelike leaves are all that remain. These are dark green and grow up to 3 feet tall and a foot wide. The common name comes from the odor released by the leaves when they are bruised or crushed.

Coastal Indians used the skunk cabbage for a variety of purposes. The Quileute and Quinault cooked and ate the roots. In the spring, when other food was scarce, skunk cabbage roots were probably easy to gather because the soil was soft. It was evidently not a favorite food because of its strong smell. The large leaves were used as baskets for gathering and drying salal and elderberries. Bears are also fond of skunk cabbage and eat the leaves, roots, and fruits. It is the roots, however, that are most eagerly sought, especially early in the spring.

Found throughout much of the Pacific Northwest.

Skunk Cabbage *Lysichitum americanum*

BUTTERCUP FAMILY Ranunculaceae

The buttercup family is large, consisting of about 1,500 species. It contains mostly perennial herbs and is well known for its wide variety of flowers. Other members of this family are described on pages 70 to 72.

BUTTERCUP *Ranunculus* species

Many of our native buttercups attract attention with brightly colored flowers that adorn roadsides and fields. Buttercups are herbs. Their floral parts are usually found in fives, with many stamens and pistils. The petals often have shiny surfaces.

Small Creeping Buttercup *Ranunculus flammula*

Small creeping buttercup maintains a low profile, growing only a few inches high. Its stems sprawl over sandy swales and send out roots at the leafy joints. The five-petaled flowers are quite small, barely a half inch across. Along the Pacific coast you'll find this buttercup occupying wet deflation plains between coastal dunes and mudflats bordering estuaries.

Found in much of North America.

Creeping Buttercup *Ranunculus repens*

Creeping buttercup is common along the Pacific coast in wet seeps and along roadside ditches. Its bright, golden, saucer-shaped flowers, for instance, are common along U.S. Highway 101 through Olympic National Park and Redwoods National Park. Creeping buttercup grows about 12 inches high. Although the stems are prostrate at the base, their ability to root at the nodes often creates a tufted appearance. The basal leaves are usually divided into three-lobed leaflets. Additional linear leaves grow on the flowering stems. Sometimes the leaves are dotted with white.

A native of Europe, it has become widely established and is found throughout much of North America.

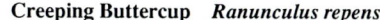

Small Creeping Buttercup   *Ranunculus flammula*

Creeping Buttercup   *Ranunculus repens*

CATTAIL FAMILY

Typhaceae

Broad-leaved Cattail

Typha latifolia

The cattail is familiar to most of us. It grows in shallow water, often to the exclusion of most other plants. You'll find it bordering shallow coastal lakes and marshes. The long, narrow leaves grow in a sheath around the flowering stems, which are between 4 and 10 feet tall. The pollen-bearing (or male) flowers and seed-producing (or female) flowers are separated on the flowering stalk. The smaller brown flowers at the top of each stalk are the pollen-bearers; the large, thickened flowers are the seed-producers, which, by the end of the summer, begin to break apart from the stalk, exuding their puffy plumes of seeds.

Cattail pollen can be used as flour, and the upper spike can be eaten in its bud stage as a vegetable. Young shoots make tasty salad greens, and the root substitutes as a potatolike food. In light of these facts, it is interesting to note that Northwest coastal Indians did not consider the cattail a primary food item. In fact, it was most often gathered as weaving material. Cattail leaves provided kneeling mats for canoes, screens for winter homes, and roof material for temporary or summer dwellings. Pack sacks and baskets were also made of this material. Perhaps the prime value of cattails today is as shelter and nesting sites for a large number of birds and other marsh wildlife.

Found from Alaska to Mexico, across southern Canada, and south along the eastern United States. It also grows in northern Africa and most of Europe and Asia.

Broad-leaved Cattail *Typha latifolia*

FIGWORT FAMILY   Scrophulariaceae

Members of the figwort family growing on cliffs and grasslands are described on pages 74 to 76, and a forest species is on page 146.

Owl Clover   *Castilleja ambigua*

Tucked amid the coarse grasses and sedges of the coastal plain is a slender-stemmed plant that grows up to 6 or 12 inches tall. The stems may be branched or spreading, and the entire plant is often covered with short hair, giving it a fuzzy appearance when one looks closely. The flower clusters are at the top of each stem and consist of bracts that are yellow- or white-tipped and pale purple flowers. The tiny flowers are tucked between the leaflike bracts.

Owl clover blooms in midsummer on salt flats such as those found at the mouth of the Chetco River in Oregon, or in the interdunal swales within the Oregon Dunes National Recreational Area. It blooms when the sand is beginning to dry and other plants are becoming dormant.

Found from British Columbia to California.

Common Monkeyflower   *Mimulus guttatus*

These bright yellow flowers are found in moist swales and along stream banks. Resembling the garden snapdragon, each flower is a two-lipped basket. The lower lip is the larger and is generally divided into three shallow lobes. Often there are spots of brown, red, purple, or maroon in the throat of the flower. Growing 2 to 24 inches tall, monkeyflower has round, irregularly lobed leaves. This monkeyflower is capable of reproducing with runners or small shoots that sprout at the base. This trait makes it especially conspicuous when it grows in moist sandy places. The runners often sprout along the waterline of a wet swale, resulting in a line of monkeyflowers that resembles a planted row.

Found in much of the Pacific Northwest and in the northern Rocky Mountains.

Similar plant: Common monkeyflower could be confused with **coast monkeyflower** (*Mimulus dentatus*), which is also found in deflation plains and swales. It, too, has yellow flowers with purple-dotted throats. In both species the leaves are opposite each other on the stem, but in the coast monkeyflower the leaves are distinctly pinnately veined, while those of common monkeyflower are usually palmately veined.

Figwort   *Scrophularia californica*

Figwort is also known as beeplant. Many travelers fail to recognize it as a wildflower. Its maroon or brown flowers are only about one-half inch long and easily escape notice. The plant itself, however, is quite tall, growing to between 2 and 5 feet in height. It is a rather coarse-appearing plant, found amid the rank growth in brushy, damp places along the coast. The flowers, each a small, two-lipped basket, are in loose panicles (flower clusters with branched stems) at the top of the plant. The leaves are opposite each other along the stem and toothed along their margins.

Found from Vancouver Island south through California.

Owl Clover   *Castilleja ambigua*   **Figwort**   *Scrophularia californica*

Common Monkeyflower   *Mimulus guttatus*

GENTIAN FAMILY Gentianaceae

Centaury *Centaurium erythraea*

Centaury dots deflation plains, damp wastelands, meadows, and swales along the Pacific coast. It grows 8 to 16 inches tall and has both tufted basal leaves and clasping elliptic stem leaves, which are opposite each other. The deep pink or nearly purple flowers are in candelabralike clusters. Each individual, tubular-shaped flower has five widely spreading lobes. Centaury's stem is square, so it does not roll easily in your fingers. Blooming throughout July and August, centaury grows in the company of sundew, labrador tea, gentian, willow, and other plants that require moist ground.

Found in much of the Pacific Northwest. Centaury was introduced from Europe.

Common Gentian *Gentiana sceptrum*

Also known as staff gentian or king's gentian, this gentian grows in wet deflation plains that stay moist through most of the summer and in coastal bogs. It does not unfold its glorious blue flowers until late summer. Even then, the funnel-shaped flower lobes scarcely appear to part. The flowers are 1 to 2 inches long and adorn plants growing 6 to 28 inches tall. The leaves are opposite each other along the entire length of the stem.

A wet meadow or bog that is covered with blooming gentian is a beautiful sight. By the time the gentian flowers appear, the rushes and sedges of the wetland have begun to turn gold or brown, the camas has replaced its blue flowers with pods of seeds, and the willow has been gnawed by insects. The deep blue of the gentian lends a splash of color to the more subtle beige hues at the end of the growing season.

Found from British Columbia to northern California.

GOOSEFOOT FAMILY Chenopodiaceae

Pickleweed *Salicornia virginica*

Coastal estuaries often appear to be bordered by mats of green. Upon closer inspection, you will see that the mats are composed of small plants resembling miniature pickles. These perennials have tough surfaces in order to resist the surge and swell of coastal tides. The plants may be either erect, about 6 to 12 inches tall, or prostrate across the tidal mud and grow from sturdy rootstocks. Look for pickleweed, also called glasswort, in the salt marshes and at the mouths of coastal rivers.

Found from Alaska to southern California.

Centaury *Centaurium erythraea*

Common Gentian *Gentiana sceptrum*

Pickleweed *Salicornia virginica*

HEATH FAMILY   Ericaceae
Members of the heath family found in brushfields are described on
pages 116 to 124.

Swamp Laurel   *Kalmia polifolia*
This very beautiful shrub has a delicate appearance and adorns boggy
meadows. It grows between 2 and 3 feet tall and has oblong, evergreen
leaves with inward-rolled edges. The pale pink blossoms bloom during the
early summer. The saucer-shaped flowers have five lobes and ten arched
stamens radiating from the center. Swamp laurel thrives in coastal bogs,
usually in the company of labrador tea.

Found from Alaska to northwest Oregon along the coast; also in the
Cascades, Sierra Nevada, and northern Rocky Mountains. At higher
elevations, the plant is much smaller.

Labrador Tea   *Ledum glandulosum*
Labrador tea graces coastal bogs and wet swales, sometimes forming a
dense thicket. It also lines damp roadside ditches, where it becomes quite
luxuriant. A beautiful shrub growing up to 4 feet tall, it has round-topped
clusters of white flowers at the ends of the branches. The leathery, evergreen
leaves have edges that are slightly rolled under. Their undersides are dotted
with small glands, hence the specific name *glandulosum*. The leaves have
a fragrant odor of their own, especially when bruised or crushed.

Found from British Columbia through central California.

HONEYSUCKLE FAMILY   Caprifoliaceae
A member of the honeysuckle family found in brushfields is described
on page 126.

Bearberry Honeysuckle   *Lonicera involucrata*
Also called twinberry, bush honeysuckle, or ink-berry, this honeysuckle
is a shrubby bush with simple, opposite leaves and tubular yellow flowers
that are sometimes tinged with pink or red. The flowers occur in pairs,
cupped in a leaflike, dark red bract and attached to the leaf axil by a long
stem. The bracts become even more conspicuous when the flowers fade and
are replaced by blue-black berries. It is the dark color of the berries that
accounts for the common name ink-berry. In fact, the ink-colored juice from
these berries was used as a dye by some of the coastal Indians. Bearberry
honeysuckle blooms from March to May.

Found throughout most of North America.

Swamp Laurel *Kalmia polifolia*

Labrador Tea *Ledum glandulosum*

Bearberry Honeysuckle
Lonicera involucrata

Bearberry Honeysuckle
Lonicera involucrata

47

IRIS FAMILY   Iridaceae

Members of the iris family found in grassy areas are described on page 80.

Golden-eyed Grass   *Sisyrinchium californicum*

The iris family is well known and loved, largely because of the large-flowered, cultivated members of the group. The smaller members of the family contained in the genus *Sisyrinchium* display the basic features of the iris, even though their flowers may superficially resemble those of the lily. Look for the smooth stems. Because of the arrangement of the ensheathing leaves at the base, they will appear to be flattened, just like those of the garden iris.

The buttery yellow flowers of the petite, golden-eyed grass dot wet, sandy places in dunes, coastal swales, bog borders, and lake margins. The stout, flattened stems grow about 12 inches tall and have somewhat shorter, irislike basal leaves. The flowers of this genus have three sepals and three petals that look alike.

Found along the coastal strip from Vancouver Island to southern California.

LILY FAMILY   Liliaceae

Other members of the lily family are described on pages 82, 128, and 148 to 152.

Common Camas   *Camassia quamash*

Common camas grows 12 to 24 inches tall and has grasslike leaves, allowing it to blend well with the sedges and grasses of the wet areas where it grows. In the spring, however, when the flowers are in bloom, it is very conspicuous. The camas has three sepals and three petals, the similar appearance of which make the flower seem to have six petals. Five of these are erect or horizontal, while the sixth turns downward.

The blue flowers of the common camas dance above wet swales and bogs with the slightest breeze. A bog covered with blooming camas in the spring tricks the observer into thinking the wet surface is a reflection of the blue sky above. It is especially spectacular in the coastal bogs of the Olympic Peninsula, where it enjoys the company of swamp laurel and labrador tea.

Camas bulbs were important to the diet of northwestern Indians. The bulbs were usually dug in late summer after the plant had gone to seed.

Found throughout much of the Pacific Northwest.

Similar plant: **Leichtlin's camas** (*Camassia leichtlinii*) has its sepals and petals arranged symmetrically. It is also common in the Pacific Northwest.

48

Golden-eyed Grass   *Sisyrinchium californicum*

Common Camas   *Camassia quamash*

Leichtlin's Camas   *Camassia leichtlinii*

49

MINT FAMILY   Labiatae

A mint found on grassy bluffs and meadows is described on page 86.

Wild Mint   *Mentha arvensis*

A fragrant herb, wild mint can be found in the deflation plains of the Clatsop Spit at the mouth of the Columbia River and in other marshes and damp spots along the coast. The leafy stems are 10 to 20 inches tall, and the round clusters of pale purple flowers are tucked in the axils of the leaves along the upper portion of the plant. Often, "suckers" sprout from the base of the plant, resulting in a bushy appearance.

You can smell the minty fragrance of this plant as you approach it. An even stronger scent is obtained if you crush a leaf. Take the stem in your fingers. It is not round, but square, and therefore does not roll very easily. Square stems are characteristic of the entire mint family.

Found across much of North America.

Wild Mint *Mentha arvensis*

ORCHID FAMILY   Orchidaceae

The tropical climates of the world are known for their large and beautiful orchids. Many people are surprised to find that a wide variety of orchids also grow in the temperate portions of North America. Although the flowers of our native orchids are usually small and inconspicuous, close examination reveals the delicate structures and beautiful patterns and colors of the most lavish tropical varieties.

An orchid that grows in coastal forests is described on page 154.

Stream Orchis   *Epipactis gigantea*

Occurring along stream banks and in moist depressions, this wildflower eludes many observers. Ornately designed, the green-and-purple flowers nonetheless blend into the surrounding vegetation. Growing from 1 to 3 feet tall, stream orchis has large (2 to 6 inches long), ovate leaves. Its flowers are arranged loosely along the upper portion of the stem.

These flowers are typical of the orchid family. Each is irregularly shaped, with three sepals and three petals. Two of these petals are alike; the third is called a lip and may be slipper-shaped, bulbous, strap-shaped, tubular, or otherwise variously shaped. It is this third petal that gives the orchid flower its unique shape. The lip of the stream orchis is concave at the base and spreads at the tip.

Found throughout much of the Pacific Northwest.

Slender Bog Orchid   *Platanthera stricta*

A spike of small green flowers helps identify this native orchid. Bog orchid has leafy stems 1 to 3 feet tall. The linear leaves occur along the entire length of the stem, but are much reduced toward the upper portion. It can be found in swampy and boggy places along the coast, but also occurs inland. The bog orchid has the characteristic design of orchid flowers, with three sepals and three petals. The petal that forms the lip in slender bog orchid is flat and fashioned into a swollen, sack-shaped spur.

Found from Alaska to southern Oregon and inland across much of western North America.

Ladies' Tresses   *Spiranthes romanzoffiana*

Resembling the finely braided hair of a well-coiffed lady, the greenish white flowers of this little orchid form a spiral twist atop a 6- to 24-inch-tall stem. The genus name, *Spiranthes*, refers to this trait, being derived from the Greek words meaning "coil" and "flower." You'll find ladies' tresses blooming in July and August in wet deflation plains and swales. Since most specimens are only 10 to 12 inches tall, you will have to get down on hands and knees to see one closely. Good places to look for ladies' tresses include the Goose Pasture at Honeyman State Park and the damp swales of the dunes on the spits at the mouths of the Umpqua and Columbia rivers.

Found from Alaska to southern California and inland across northern North America.

Stream Orchis *Epipactis gigantea*

Slender Bog Orchid
Platanthera stricta

Ladies' Tresses
Spiranthes romanzoffiana

53

PARSLEY FAMILY   Umbelliferae

Other members of the parsley family are described on pages 16 and 88 to 92.

Water Parsley   *Oenanthe sarmentosa*

Water parsley's prolific growth produces a pale white halo over many coastal marshes and roadside ditches. The stems grow up to 4 feet long and branch into a tangled mass. The compound leaves have coarsely toothed leaflets. The tiny white flowers are borne in a tight, round-topped cluster called an umbel, characteristic of the parsley family.

As might be expected of a water plant, water parsley has thick, juicy stems. Because of its similarity to the poisonous **water hemlock** (*Cicuta douglasii*) and **poison hemlock** (*Conium maculatum*), no attempt should be made to eat or taste any part of this plant. All three plants grow in moist sites.

Found in the Pacific states from Alaska to central California.

PEA FAMILY   Leguminosae

Members of the pea family found on coastal beaches and dunes are described on pages 18 to 20; those found in brushfields are described on page 130.

Bird's-foot Trefoil   *Lotus corniculatus*

Bird's-foot trefoil is a brightly colored plant that may be found in moist wasteland areas, such as roadsides, ditches, pastures, and fields. Compact clusters of yellow flowers top the 10- to 20-inch-tall stems, which are as apt to lie along the ground as to be upright. The leaves appear to be sessile and have five hairy leaflets. The bright yellow flowers make a colorful display in midsummer, giving way to slender pods later in the season.

Found throughout the Pacific Northwest. Orginally a European plant, it is now a naturalized United States resident.

Marsh Clover   *Trifolium wormskioldii*

The clovers are distinctive herbs characterized by compound leaves of three leaflets and flowers that are clustered into tight round balls. Many clovers are extremely important cash crops, grown for pasture and hay. Like commercial varieties, native clovers are extremely rich in nutrients. Many small rodents, especially chipmunks and ground squirrels, feast on both the leaves and the blossoms. In addition, the nectar-rich flowers are sought by bees, which pollinate the blossoms in return for the nectar.

Spreading by creeping rootstocks, marsh clover, also called spring-bank clover, may grow erect, though more often it sprawls across the sand in sunny openings. It is noticeable mainly because of its round, showy clusters of flowers. These are purple or red, sometimes tipped in white. Marsh clover occurs along fresh or salt marshes or in sandy depressions and dunes.

Found from British Columbia south to California and Mexico.

Water Parsley *Oenanthe sarmentosa*

Poison Hemlock *Conium maculatum*

Bird's-foot Trefoil *Lotus corniculatus*

Marsh Clover *Trifolium wormskioldii*

PITCHER PLANT FAMILY   Sarraceniaceae

Cobra Lily   *Darlingtonia californica*
Scattered along the northern coast are small seeps, where you will find some very interesting and unique plants. Some seeps are open and sunny, looking at first like wet meadows. Others are partially shaded. Some may be merely soggy or spongy and dry out by the end of the summer.

One of the most interesting and conspicuous plants growing in these wetlands is the cobra lily. It has tubular, pitcherlike leaves filled with enzymatic fluid. This liquid aids the plant in dissolving insects and other small creatures that become trapped inside the leaves. These leaves are 1 to 2 feet tall. In the early summer a flowering stalk appears, extending about 6 inches higher than the leaves and bearing a single, nodding flower with five purple petals and five yellow sepals. The cobra lily gets its name from the cobra-like appearance of the upper portion of the leaves. Another common name for it is pitcher plant.

Found in coastal areas from central Oregon to northwestern California.

PRIMROSE FAMILY   Primulaceae
Another member of the primrose family is described on page 96.

Sea Milkwort   *Glaux maritima*
To find the delicate pink flowers of the sea milkwort, you must venture into saltwater sloughs and tidewater flats. There, it grows amid the reeds and sedges so common along coastal waterways. A fleshy plant, sea milkwort grows 10 to 12 inches tall and has pale pink, bell-shaped flowers tucked in the axils of the small, oblong leaves.

Found in much of North America. A cosmopolitan plant, it is also found in coastal areas and alkaline waterways in Europe and Asia.

Cobra Lily *Darlingtonia californica*

Cobra Lily *Darlingtonia californica*

Sea Milkwort *Glaux maritima*

Sea Milkwort *Glaux maritima*

57

ROSE FAMILY   Rosaceae

Additional members of the rose family can be found on pages 24, 98, and 132 to 138.

Burnet   *Sanguisorba officinalis*

Burnet grows in bogs, wet seeps, and marshes along the coast, often in the company of camas and bog laurel. Burnet is conspicuous not for its individual flowers, but rather for the eye-catching appearance of its oblong cluster of rose or purple blossoms. These are grouped together at the end of the stems, somewhat resembling a head of grain. The flower clusters are 1 to 2 inches long and are on stems 4 to 24 inches tall. The pinnately compound leaves have toothed leaflets and are hidden amid the other marsh vegetation. While burnet may not be very common, it is plentiful in local areas where it does occur. Thus, the overall effect can be very striking. The burnt red clusters of flowers wave above the marsh grasses and sedges.

Found from Alaska south along the coast and in the mountains to northwestern California; also in northern Europe and Asia.

Douglas Spirea   *Spiraea douglasii*

Also called western spirea, hardhack, and steeple-bush, Douglas spirea is a conspicuous, pink-flowered shrub commonly found along roadside ditches and lake margins. It is a beautiful little shrub that grows 3 to 6 feet tall and has oblong, toothed leaves. The flowers bloom in midsummer in pyramid-shaped clusters that appear fuzzy because the numerous stamens in each flower are longer than the other floral parts. The flowers are pleasantly scented, and their fragrance further enhances the beauty of the plant.

Found from southern Alaska south along the coast to northern California and inland to British Columbia and Idaho.

Burnet *Sanguisorba officinalis*

Burnet *Sanguisorba officinalis*

Douglas Spirea *Spiraea douglasii*

Douglas Spirea *Spiraea douglasii*

ST. JOHN'S WORT FAMILY　　　　Hypericaceae

Tinker's Penny　　　　*Hypericum anagalloides*
If you trek into boggy spots or wet sandy areas, you may find yourself walking on tiny yellow flowers with glistening, dark green leaves. This is tinker's penny, also known as bog St. John's wort.

Even when erect, they are not very tall—usually only 6 inches or less. Half-inch, ovate leaves straddle the stems in pairs. The bright golden flowers are about one-half inch in diameter and have five petals. The shiny leaves always appear wet. This is mostly due to the glistening glands on the leaves, not morning dew. However, if you plan to look for this dainty flower yourself, you should plan on getting your feet wet. It grows best where the ground is saturated with water.

Tinker's penny adapts well to cool, moist garden nooks and makes a pleasant addition to a native garden.

Found from British Columbia south to Baja California.

SUNDEW FAMILY　　　　Droseraceae

Sundew　　　　*Drosera rotundifolia*
Sundews are lowly plants, barely a few inches across. Their small size allows them to be easily overlooked. Once seen, however, they can be mistaken for no other native plant. Their round leaves form a rosette that hugs the damp ground. Indeed, to get a good look at them you will need to get more than your feet wet. Kneel down on your knees to get closer. These little leaves are covered with sticky gland-tipped hairs in which small insects such as gnats and mosquitoes become entrapped. The moist appearance that these secreting glands give the leaves undoubtedly led to the plant's common name, since the leaf seems perpetually laden with dew. Once an insect has landed on the leaf, the small hairs tip inward, and the insect is digested by enzymes secreted by the leaf. Even less frequently seen than the plant itself are its tiny white flowers, which are borne on slender 5- or 6-inch-tall stems. Sundews may grow in the soggy edge of a marsh or lake, in a coastal seep or bog, or in a perpetually moist deflation plain.

Both the sundew and cobra lily (page 56) are sometimes called insectivorous or carnivorous plants because they absorb nutrients from small insects or other animal material. The extra nutrients derived from these tiny creatures help the plants to survive. These plants grow in sites such as bogs, where the normal soil nutrients are either deficient or simply difficult to absorb from the soil.

Found in the northern reaches of North America, Europe, and Asia. In North America, it is considered to be circumpolar. It also extends south along the Pacific and Atlantic coasts and into the Cascade Mountains and the northern Rockies.

Tinker's Penny *Hypericum anagalloides*

Sundew *Drosera rotundifolia*

SUNFLOWER FAMILY   Compositae

See page 102 for a description of the sunflower family. Other members of the group are described on pages 26 to 30, 102 to 110, 140, and 158.

Brass Buttons   *Cotula coronopifolia*

These yellow flowers deserve their common name, as they do indeed resemble buttons. The low-growing plant has stems that are barely 12 inches long and may be almost prostrate. The oblong leaves clasp the stem, and the lower ones may be deeply cleft. The flower heads, about one-half inch wide, are flattened but slightly raised in the center. There are no ray flowers, the compact disk being formed by tubular flowers. Brass buttons may be found blooming in tidal marshes, wet beaches, deflation plains, and bogs. The flowers appear during the early part of the summer.

Found along the Pacific coast from British Columbia through California, as well as along the Atlantic coast of North America and in the Southern Hemisphere. Brass buttons is a native of South Africa.

Gumweed   *Grindelia integrifolia*

Gumweed is best recognized by the cup-shaped base of the flower head, the outward curving bracts below the flower head that appear to have been coated with varnish, and the gummy substance associated with the flower head. In fact, when a new flower head opens, it is almost completely covered by this sticky, white substance. The large yellow floral head (2 inches across is not uncommon) consists of both ray and disk flowers. Gumweed grows 2 to 3 feet tall, and each plant contains many showy flower heads, so a cluster of these leafy plants is quite striking. Look for it along open beaches, roadside ditches, and saltwater marshes. Gumweed blooms in August and September, although in some northern locations it may still be seen blooming in early October.

Found from southern Alaska through northern California.

A gumweed commonly found on beaches is described on page 28.

Jaumea   *Jaumea carnosa*

Jaumea's succulent leaves and stems spread horizontally across the ground, forming a loose mat. The narrow leaves are opposite each other, clasping the stem at the base. A single yellow flower head sits on its own somewhat erect stem, which is 3 to 4 inches tall. Jaumea blooms from June through October. Look for it in tidal areas, usually sprawled across the inlets and peninsulas carved by the ebb and flow of the ocean.

Found from Vancouver Island to southern California. A small genus of only about nine species, jaumea has only this representative on our Pacific coast. Other members of this genus occur in Mexico, South America, and Africa.

Brass Buttons   *Cotula coronopifolia*   **Gumweed**   *Grindelia integrifolia*

Jaumea   *Jaumea carnosa*

SWEET GALE FAMILY   Myricaceae

The sweet gale family is recognizable by the aromatic fragrance that exudes from its leaves when they are crushed or bruised. These coastal shrubs are related to several well-known spices, including cloves and allspice. Wax myrtle is often planted for landscaping and graces many coastal picnic sites, waysides, and campgrounds.

Wax Myrtle   *Myrica californica*

A shrub or small tree between 3 and 30 feet tall, wax myrtle is identified by its shiny, leathery, evergreen leaves and its clusters of nutlike, wax-covered fruits. The flowers are quite inconspicuous, looking like tiny, green catkins. It is the waxy fruit that is noticeable. The 4-inch elliptic leaves have finely serrated margins.

Found along the coast from Washington to California.

WATER LILY FAMILY   Nymphacaceae

Yellow Pond Lily   *Nuphar luteum*

These yellow bowl-shaped flowers adorn many of the sloughs and intertidal and interdunal ponds and lakes along the Pacific coast. A thick rootstock anchors the yellow pond lily to the mud below and large leaves float alongside. The leaves are also conspicuous. They are rounded, heart-shaped at their base, and often 12 inches or more across.

This plant was known by the inland Klamath Indians as *wokas* and was harvested using dugout canoes. The ripened pods were pulled, stored, dried, and roasted. The harvesting of *wokas* seed was cause for celebrating among the Klamaths. Other coastal Indians used this plant medicinally. The Quinault gathered the roots along the river, heated them, and applied them to the body to relieve pain, especially rheumatism. This plant is also important to a vast number of aquatic insects and other small creatures that seek shelter under its protective leaves. You will find insect eggs attached to the underside. Here, the eggs are kept moist while incubating, and the newly hatched insects have a ready food supply.

Found throughout most of western North America.

Wax Myrtle *Myrica californica*   **Wax Myrtle** *Myrica californica*

Yellow Pond Lily *Nuphar luteum*

Cliffs and Grasslands

Many of the Pacific coast headlands are underlain by dark basalt. These rocky promontories may be carpeted with a dense cover of grass or brush on their southern slopes, before dropping steeply into the sea. In the spring and early summer, when moisture collects in the thin mantle of soil, myriad flowers appear. The brightly colored stonecrop nestles in nooks and crannies, its succulent leaves storing moisture during the early summer to be used when the soil dries. The columbine, larkspur, footsteps-of-spring, thrift, and mission bells herald the coming summer. Later, as the slopes begin to dry, a fresh crop of flowers appear; wild carrot, self-heal, pearly everlasting, daisy, and goldenrod are but a few. These headlands offer spectacular views of the ocean surf as well as an excellent place to look for wildflowers.

The coastal vegetation gradually changes as one travels southward. Forested slopes dominate the shoreline of Vancouver Island and the Washington coast. Basalt headlands punctuate the Oregon coast; their southern slopes begin to be covered with grassland rather than forest, as you travel southward. Farther south still, open, grassy slopes are more frequently encountered, along with forests that crawl down ravines toward the ocean. The warmer, drier climate and the steep mountain slopes and bluffs influence this change of scene.

BARBERRY FAMILY Berberidaceae

Oregon Grape *Berberis nervosa*

These bright golden flowers, also known as mahonia, barberry, holly grape, little Oregon grape, and long-leaved Oregon grape, may be found in late April, May, and June on open bluffs and forest borders. You'll recognize the shiny leaves of eleven to twenty-one holly-shaped leaflets. Growing up to 3 feet tall, this species spreads readily from underground, horizontal stems. The purple, grapelike berries appear by the end of the summer.

Found from British Columbia to central California.

Similar plant: The type of **Oregon grape** (*Berberis aquifolium*) known as the state flower of Oregon is more common inland. It grows up to 6 feet tall and has leaves with five to nine leaflets. It is widely planted for landscaping along roadsides, in parks, and around office buildings.

BUCKTHORN FAMILY Rhamnaceae

Point Reyes Creeper *Ceanothus gloriosus*

Also known as glory mat, this prostrate, sprawling plant trails over rocks and beaches and is quite conspicuous when in bloom. You can identify it by its thick, leathery, glossy-green hollylike leaves and its distinctive lavender or blue flower clusters. Although the individual flowers are small, the showy clusters are bright and easy to spot. The five petals of each flower are elongated into a claw or spoon shape. The stamens extend beyond the petals, giving the flowers a fuzzy appearance.

This charming plant makes a pleasant addition to a native garden, where it makes an attractive ground cover.

Found along much of the California coast.

A *Ceanothus* that grows in brushfields is described on page 114.

Oregon Grape   *Berberis nervosa*

Oregon Grape   *Berberis nervosa*

Oregon Grape   *Berberis aquifolium*

Point Reyes Creeper   *Ceanothus gloriosus*

69

BUTTERCUP FAMILY

Ranunculaceae

Columbine

Aquilegia formosa

The columbine is one of the more common and beloved wildflowers in the Northwest. It is also one of our most beautiful. A 2- or 4-foot stem supports the showy, nodding flowers. These are formed from five prolonged petals that are turned backward and upward to form crimson spurs, or sacs, while the forward portions form yellow blades. This columbine can be found from sea level nearly to timberline. It grows in a variety of soil types but does best along woodland borders. The colorful blossoms appear in April and May, but a few can usually still be found toward the end of the summer.

This columbine provides a charming addition to flower gardens and is very easy to start from seed. You can collect the seeds in late summer and plant them in midwinter. They will sprout the first spring and send up flowering stems the second summer. Then they will provide color for your garden for many years to come.

Found throughout the Pacific states.

Field Larkspur

Delphinium menziesii

Larkspurs range over much of North America. Many kinds are difficult to tell apart; however, the group as a whole is easy to identify. Larkspurs are herbaceous plants with palmately lobed leaves and irregularly shaped purple flowers that are in clusters at the upper tip of the flowering stem. A long, backward-protruding spur is formed by one of the sepals. It is this distinctive shape that makes larkspurs easy to identify.

This species, which grows up to 2 feet tall, has leaves that are deeply cleft into three to five main parts, and these are divided again. Even though the basal leaves are deeply cleft, they have a round outline. Only a few flowers are clustered at the tip of each stem. These flowers are a dark purple, except for the upper petals, which are usually white or lined with purple. Look for field larkspur on coastal bluffs, where it may be found in the company of the wallflower, cow parsnip, and blue violet.

Found from British Columbia to California.

Columbine   *Aquilegia formosa*

Field Larkspur   *Delphinium menziesii*

BUTTERCUP
Ranunculus species

Buttercups are among the most common and well-known wildflowers. They are recognized by their shiny or waxy yellow petals, of which there are usually five. Two species common on damp sites are described on page 38. Two species found among the grasses of coastal headlands, meadows, and fields, and often encountered along the Pacific coast, are the western field buttercup and the California buttercup.

California Buttercup
Ranunculus californicus

California buttercup is easily recognized because it deviates from the normal buttercup pattern of five petals. Instead, it has eight to sixteen petals on each flower. Although it grows up to 2 feet tall in sheltered areas, the form found on coastal headlands has a much shorter stem. It appears to sprawl amid the wind-blown grasses of ocean slopes, and therefore appears prostrate.

Found in Oregon and California.

Field Buttercup
Ranunculus occidentalis

Field buttercup has several stems 4 to 20 inches tall. The lower leaves are usually three-lobed, each lobe again being shallowly lobed or toothed. The yellow flowers have five narrow petals and are about an inch in diameter.

Found mostly along the coast, from Alaska to California.

EVENING PRIMROSE FAMILY
Onagraceae

Other members of the evening primrose family are described on pages 12 and 116.

Clarkia
Clarkia unguiculata

Also called farewell-to-spring, clarkias are showy, springtime flowers with four brightly colored petals that are distinctively shaped. In this clarkia, they are very narrow at the base, expanding at the tip, so that they are shaped like a short-handled spoon. The blossoms range in color from pale pink to lavender. This clarkia grows 1 to 2 feet tall and has narrow lance-shaped or ovate leaves. When a hillside of clarkias are blooming and swaying in the coastal breeze, it becomes a wave of color.

The genus *Clarkia* was named after Captain William Clark of the Lewis and Clark Expedition to the Northwest in 1804. Clark and Meriwether Lewis collected nearly 200 specimens of new plants. Many place and plant names honor these intrepid explorers.

Found along the length of the California coast and also in the Sierra Nevada foothills.

California Buttercup   *Ranunculus californicus*

Field Buttercup   Clarkia
Ranunculus occidentalis   *Clarkia unguiculata*

73

FIGWORT FAMILY Scrophulariaceae

Members of the figwort family growing in wetlands are described on page 42, and a forest species is on page 146.

Coast Paintbrush *Castilleja affinis*

You will have to get down on hands and knees and look carefully to see the flowers of paintbrush. What appear to be "flowers" are actually bracts, like the conspicuous part of the poinsettia and the dogwood. These bracts shelter the true blossoms. If you fold them back, you'll find small, tubular flowers that are two-lipped. They are usually subdued colors of green, orange, or red. It is the larger bract with its bright colors that attracts attention and makes the paintbrush group so colorful.

Overlooking the ocean from basalt headlands, bluffs, and partially stabilized dunes, coast paintbrush lends its beauty to rugged sections of the Pacific coastline. Blooming through most of the summer months, this is the most common paintbrush found along our coast. Its loosely clustered stems are woody at the base and grow 5 to 25 inches tall. The hairy bracts are tipped with scarlet, often with a band of yellow below. The flower itself, tucked within the bract, is pale green or red.

Found from Washington to northern California.

Similar plant: **Seaside paintbrush** (*Castilleja latifolia*) is very showy, with rounded or oblong leaves. The stems and leaves are densely hairy. It is found along the central and northern California coast.

Foxglove *Digitalis purpurea*

Foxglove is a beautiful, very showy plant along roadsides and other recently disturbed areas. Growing 2 to 6 feet tall, its hairy leaves are toothed and oblong. Foxglove is a biennial, meaning that it requires two years to complete its life cycle. A rosette is formed during the first growing season; the flower-bearing stem appears the second year. It is the flowers that attract attention. They are basket-shaped, from 1 to 2 inches long, and are concentrated along the upper portion of the stem. Hanging downward, they are purple or sometimes white, with dark spots on the inner lining.

Foxglove is a native of Europe that was transported to North America by early settlers, either as a garden plant or for its medicinal properties. It was gathered extensively in Oregon and Washington during the First World War to make digitalis, a drug used to treat heart ailments. (The drug is now manufactured synthetically, rather than taken from the wild plant.) Foxglove readily covers disturbed sites, such as road banks and recently logged areas. It also invades grazing pastures, where it is considered a pest by farmers because it is toxic to livestock.

Found on the west side of the Cascade-Sierra divide from British Columbia to southern California.

Coast Paintbrush   *Castilleja affinis*

Foxglove   *Digitalis purpurea*

Seaside Paintbrush   *Castilleja latifolia*

Bush Monkeyflower
Mimulus aurantiacus

The bright orange or scarlet flowers of this monkeyflower attract attention along coastal bluffs and cliffs, in steep brushfields, and in open woodlands along State Highway 1, at Point Reyes National Seashore, and at Whale's Head on the southern Oregon coast. The trumpet-shaped flowers have the characteristic monkeyflower shape, i.e., the outer part of the trumpet flaring apart, with three lobes pointing downward and two pointing up. The shrub may grow as tall as 6 feet (although 2 to 3 feet is more common) and is covered with sticky, dark green leaves.

Found from southwestern Oregon through central California.

Parentucellia
Parentucellia viscosa

Erect, leafy stems with spikes of bright yellow two-lipped flowers mark this plant, which frequents grassy coastal overlooks. It grows 8 to 18 inches tall. The flowers are tubular, with a three-lobed lower lip and the upper lip shaped to form a hood. This colorful plant blooms from April through June.

Originally from Europe and considered a weed; now found throughout much of the Pacific states.

FLAX FAMILY
Linaceae

Wild Flax
Linum bienne

The pale blue flowers of wild flax, barely ½ inch in diameter, wave on slender, 6- to 12-inch-tall stems tucked in the grasses of coastal bluffs and meadows. The dainty, five-petaled flowers are not conspicuous; however, they are often quite plentiful and therefore attract attention. Wild flax is a perennial, with several stems bearing narrow, linear leaves along their length. Look for wild flax along the roadsides at Cape Blanco and in the grassy coastal meadows of Redwoods National Park, where it blooms from April through much of the summer.

Found from central California north into southern Oregon.

Bush Monkeyflower *Mimulus aurantiacus*

Parentucellia *Parentucellia viscosa*

Wild Flax *Linum bienne*

77

GOURD FAMILY

Cucuribitaceae

Wild Cucumber

Marah oreganus

Wild cucumber clambers over coastal vegetation, its tendrils (thin, coiling stems or modified leaves) attaching to other plants for support. The broad, rough-textured leaves are lobed and grow out from the long, vinelike stem. Wild cucumber blooms in April, May, and June. There are two types of flowers. The pollen-bearing flowers are in a long-stemmed cluster, while the seed-bearing flower is solitary and is found in the leaf axil. The green fruit resembles a small round cucumber and is about 3 inches long. Its surface is covered with soft bristles.

Other common names for wild cucumber are big root and old-man-in-the-ground. These names refer to the large, woody root. Specimens weighing more than 20 pounds have been found. It is the large size of this root that allows the rapid above-ground growth of wild cucumber in an area that has been recently cleared or otherwise disturbed.

Found from southern British Columbia to California.

Wild Cucumber *Marah oreganus*

79

IRIS FAMILY Iridaceae

Most people recognize a wild iris because they have see the cultivated variety. The large, showy flowers have three sepals that turn backward or outward, while the three petals are erect. The cultivated plants have flowers bred for almost any color imaginable; however, the native coastal varieties are usually various shades of blue or purple. Occasionally, cream-colored or yellow specimens occur. They grow along roadsides and on open grassy bluffs, either in full sun or partial shade.

A member of the iris family found in wetlands is described on page 48.

Wild Iris *Iris tenax*

Wild iris, also called blue flag, grows in open, grassy areas. Usually a single violet or purple (sometimes white) flower is found on each 10- to 20-inch-tall stem. Numerous basal leaves and leaflike bracts along the flowering stem help distinguish this species. The leaves are extremely narrow, almost grasslike, rarely ¼ inch wide.

Iris leaves were gathered by coastal Indians for the long, silky fiber found along the margin of each leaf. Scraped clean with a mussel shell, they were twisted and braided. A great amount of work was required to make cord or rope from iris; nonetheless, it was a prime fiber for making fishnets, bags, and small snares.

Found in Oregon and Washington.

Similar plant: In open woods along the California and southern Oregon coasts you are most apt to find another wild iris, *Iris douglasiana*. This iris also has blue or purple flowers. Although its leaves, too, are grasslike, they are usually much wider than those of *Iris tenax*, being ¼ to ½ inch wide.

Blue-eyed Grass *Sisyrinchium bellum*

Blue-eyed grass has stout, flattened stems and linear, irislike leaves. The flowers, with three blue sepals and three blue petals, look much like a small lily. The centers of the flowers are yellow. Blooming through much of the spring, blue-eyed grass may be found with the grasses and other spring-flowering plants of bluffs and meadows overlooking the shore.

Found along much of the Pacific coast and across northern North America.

LEADWORT FAMILY Plumbaginaceae

Thrift *Armeria maritima*

Found on bluffs and terraces along the ocean, thrift, also called sea pink, has compact, round clusters of pink flowers that dance wildly in the sea breeze. The narrow leaves are tufted at the base of the flowering stem, which grows 4 to 20 inches tall. Thrift blooms from April through August, so is seen by many coastal visitors.

Thrift has found its way into many domestic yards and gardens as a charming addition to a rock garden.

Found along the Pacific and Atlantic coasts of North America.

Wild Iris   *Iris tenax*

Blue-eyed Grass   *Sisyrinchium bellum*

Thrift   *Armeria maritima*

81

LILY FAMILY Liliaceae

Other members of the lily family are described on pages 48, 128, and 148 to 152.

Harvest Brodiaea *Brodiaea coronaria*

Masses of funnel-shaped purple or violet flowers mark this brodiaea. Found on grassy bluffs along the coast, brodiaeas usually command a magnificent ocean vista. You'll find them amid the drying grasses of late spring to early summer. The cluster of flowers, each on its own short stalk, is on a stem 2 to 10 inches tall. The entire plant somewhat resembles a candelabra.

Brodiaea bulbs were important in the diet of many coastal Indians, who dug them up with pointed sticks. The bulbs were eaten both raw and cooked.

Found from Vancouver Island south through California.

Similar plant: **Blue dicks** (*Brodiaea capitata*) is found along the southern Oregon and California coasts. Its deep blue flowers, however, are tightly clustered together, and the plant is much larger, growing between 1 to 2 feet tall.

Mission Bells *Fritillaria affinis*

You must look early in the season to find this little lily hiding amid the grasses of coastal headlands, where it thrives in the well-drained soils. Growing 1 to 2 feet tall, this plant, also called rice-root lily or checker lily, has showy, brown or maroon flowers that appear in early spring. One to several flowers adorn a single stalk. They are bell-shaped and often mottled with purple spots. The underground bulb is covered with tiny bulblets that resemble grains of rice, giving rise to one of its common names, rice-root lily.

Found from British Columbia to California.

Harvest Brodiaea   *Brodiaea coronaria*

Mission Bells   *Fritillaria affinis*

MALLOW FAMILY Malvaceae

The mallow family is widespread and contains many plants that are grown commercially, cotton being one of the more important. The large, showy flowers of many mallow species have made them popular in the garden as well. The hibiscus and common hollyhock are included in this category.

Bluff Mallow *Sidalcea hirtipes*

Found on coastal bluffs and grasslands, this mallow blooms in late June and early July. A stout plant with hairy, leafy steams, it grows about 3 feet tall. The five-petaled pink or lavender flowers are clustered near the tip of the stems and make an eye-catching dash of color amid the rank grasses that surround it.

Found along the Washington and Oregon coasts.

Wild Hollyhock *Sidalcea malvaeflora*

Also called checkerbloom, the wild hollyhock is fairly common on grassy bluffs and meadows. It is a perennial, with stems and leaves covered with stiff hairs. It grows luxuriantly up to 3 feet tall in moist sheltered areas, or lies nearly prostrate where it is buffeted by the wind. The five-petaled pink flowers are borne in terminal racemes, meaning the flowers at the lower end of the cluster bloom first. Look for wild hollyhock in May and early June growing on coastal prairies in the company of red maids, blue-eyed grass, wild iris, and gold fields.

Bluff Mallow *Sidalcea hirtipes*

Wild Hollyhock *Sidalcea malvaeflora*

MINT FAMILY Labiatae

A mint found in wetland areas is described on page 50.

Self-Heal *Prunella vulgaris*

Self-heal is found in moist shaded areas or meadows. It grows 4 to 12 inches tall and has opposite oblong or ovate leaves that are 1 to 3 inches long. Small pink or purple flowers grow in dense terminal spikes that are an inch or more tall.

The name self-heal comes from the plant's supposed value as a remedy for a variety of ailments, especially the common sore throat. Its ability to adapt to new conditions is reflected in the specific name *vulgaris*, meaning "common." There are several subspecies. The native variety is an erect plant, while the European variety, which also occurs along the coast, is dwarf or prostrate. It forms a blue carpet in the otherwise manicured lawns of several of our coastal state parks.

Found throughout most of North America.

MUSTARD FAMILY Cruciferae

The mustard group is fairly large and contains a variable assortment of plants. Some, like the cabbage, turnip, and radish, are of economic value. Others are more often thought of as weeds growing alongside roadsides and in abandoned fields. As a group, they are identified by alternate leaves and a characteristic flower. There are four sepals and four petals, which spread opposite each other to form a cross (the Latin name for the family is Cruciferae, referring to the cross formed by the opposite petals). There are six stamens, two of which are shorter than the other four. This floral pattern is typical of mustard flowers and helps to identify the group.

A mustard found on the open beach is described on page 16.

Wallflower *Erysimum capitatum*

The orange and yellow of wallflowers add bright color to rocky cliffs and grassy bluffs. This wallflower is a stout, coarse plant, the hairy stems of which grow 1 to 3 feet tall. Narrow, linear leaves extend along the stem and are 3 to 6 inches long. It is the cluster of flowers, however, that attracts attention. The cluster is round-topped, 3 to 4 inches in diameter, and consists of bright burnt red, yellow, or maroon flowers.

Found throughout much of western North America.

Wild Radish *Raphanus sativus*

The wild radish is a conspicuous plant along roadsides and fields and is common at the edge of coastal beaches, in campgrounds and waysides, and along grassy openings. It is a coarse plant, with branching stems nearly 3 feet tall. The plant is loaded with blossoms, giving it the appearance of a flowering bush. The flowers range in color from cream to pale pink or purple. They bloom through most of the summer, making them prominent on the coastal scene.

Found throughout much of the western states.

Self-Heal *Prunella vulgaris*

Wallflower *Erysimum capitatum*

Wild Radish *Raphanus sativus*

Wild Radish *Raphanus sativus*

87

PARSLEY FAMILY   Umbelliferae

The parsley family contains some 3,000 species of plants, including well-known aromatic specimens widely used as spices. These include celery, parsley, and carrot. The family is fairly distinctive because the flowers are in groupings called umbels, meaning the individual flower stems originate from a common point, much like the ribs of an umbrella. The relative length of these stems determines whether the flower cluster is flat-topped or rounded. The parsley family is well represented in the coastal flora. While many kinds grow in the well-drained soils of grassy slopes and cliffs, others may be found on the beach (page 16) or in wetlands (page 54).

Angelica   *Angelica hendersonii*

Henderson's angelica grows 3 to 6 feet tall and has stout, hollow stems. The pinnately compound leaves have petioles (leaf stems) that closely sheath the main stem. These leaves are green above, but covered by a dense coat of woolly hairs beneath. The white flowers are in round-topped umbels and each flower in the cluster is of equal size.

Found from southern Washington to central California.

Similar plant: **Seacoast angelica** (*Angelica lucida*) is very similar, but the leaves lack the woolly covering on the undersides. It is found along the entire length of the Pacific coast as well as on the Atlantic and Siberian coasts.

Angelica *Angelica hendersonii*

Wild Carrot   *Daucus carota*

By the end of the summer, the grasses of coastal headlands and fields turn a golden brown. Few flowers remain in bloom. The wild carrot, however, is in its prime, waving parasols of tiny white flowers in the breeze. All the flowers are white, except the central flower, which is a deep rose color. From above, the round flower clusters resemble a carefully embroidered doily of lace 2 to 3 inches across. This pattern gives rise to the common name Queen Anne's lace.

A stout, hairy plant with finely divided carrotlike leaves, wild carrot reaches up to 3 feet tall. It grows from a fleshy taproot, which plainly has a carrot odor. In fact, it is from this humble plant that all domestic carrots have been derived. Wild carrot is generally a biennial, meaning the first year only a clump of leaves appear close to the ground. Not until the second year does the flower stalk grow.

Found throughout most of North America, wild carrot is originally a native of Europe that has become widely established over much of North America.

Similar plant: The native **American carrot** (*Daucus pusillus*) is much smaller, barely reaching 12 inches in height. Its flower clusters are only about an inch across. An annual plant, it too is common in dry, open areas along the coast.

Cow Parsnip   *Heracleum lanatum*

Cow parsnip is one of the most easily recognized members of the parsley family. Its large size makes it impossible to overlook. The stout stems grow 4 or 5 feet tall, although they occasionally grow even taller. The stems are not the only large part of this plant; the leaves, divided into three deeply toothed leaflets, are also large. They grow 3 to 10 inches across and their general shape resembles rhubarb. The white flowers are clustered into flat-topped heads 5 to 12 inches across. You'll find cow parsnip blooming in moist spots and grassy coastal slopes during the early part of the summer.

Coastal Indians sought out cow parsnip in the spring. The young tops were consumed raw and the stems eaten later in the summer, sometimes with seal oil. The ribs of the large flower clusters were used for making small baskets.

Found in much of North America and also in Siberia.

Wild Carrot   *Daucus carota*

Cow Parsnip   *Heracleum lanatum*

Cow Parsnip   *Heracleum lanatum*

Spring Gold   *Lomatium utriculatum*

One of the earliest plants to bloom in the spring, you can find spring gold's clusters of golden flowers dotting well-drained slopes and bluffs in March. The leaves are dissected into many small lacy segments. The umbels of yellow flowers are tucked close to the ground. Spring gold continues to bloom through the spring months; however, the flowers are on taller stems (up to 12 inches tall) and tend to become lost amid the faster-growing surrounding grasses. Since spring gold grows best on rocky bluffs, it usually commands scenic, windswept vistas. Wherever you find it, you will also be treated to an ocean view.

The genus *Lomatium* is known for its long taproot. Most Indian tribes of the Northwest used the roots extensively for food and taught this use to early explorers and settlers. The journals of Lewis and Clark record buying *Lomatium* roots from local Indians as they traveled across North America to the Pacific.

Found from British Columbia south through California. Other members of this genus are scattered across the northern Great Plains and in the Rockies, Cascades, and Sierra Nevada.

Footsteps-of-Spring   *Sanicula arctopoides*

Blooming on exposed bluffs and beaches in March and April, footsteps-of-spring, also called snake-root and yellow-mats, is well named. Remaining low to the ground, its leaves and stems form a rosette-type arrangement about a foot across. The leaves are divided into three deeply lobed segments. The rather inconspicuous yellow flowers are grouped on compact umbels. The foliage of footsteps-of-spring has a yellow-green tinge, allowing it to stand out a bit amid the fresh green foliage of most early spring plants.

Found from Vancouver Island south along the coast to southern California.

Spring Gold *Lomatium utriculatum*

Footsteps-of-Spring *Sanicula arctopoides*

PHLOX FAMILY

Polemoniaceae

Blue Gilia

Gilia capitata

An erect, annual plant, this gilia grows on open slopes and meadows. It is also called globe gilia because of its round floral clusters. The deep blue or lavender blossoms are in dense, round clusters (containing as many as 100 or more individual flowers) that are about an inch across. Blue gilia grows from 10 to 24 inches tall and has 1- to 4-inch-long leaves, divided into deeply notched, narrow lobes.

The genus *Gilia* contains from forty to fifty species of plants, of which more than half occur in California. This gilia was first collected by the early botanical explorer David Douglas, during his stay at Fort Vancouver. Douglas was one of the first botanists to travel and collect specimens in the Pacific states. Sent by the Horticultural Society of London, Douglas was stationed at the Hudson's Bay Company's Fort Vancouver from 1825 to 1827 and again in 1830. From there he traveled to Monterey, California, where he worked until 1832. During this time, he sent a great number of seeds back to England. Native North American plants soon graced many English gardens.

Found from British Columbia to central California.

PINK FAMILY

Caryophyllaceae

A member of the pink family found on coastal beaches is described on page 22.

Field Chickweed

Cerastium arvense

These showy, white flowers, often with petals nearly an inch across, grow on bluffs and grasslands along the coast. The deeply notched petals produce an ornate appearance. Several stems 3 to 20 inches tall emerge from the plant base, giving chickweed a tufted appearance. The lance-shaped leaves are glandular, making them slightly sticky. Chickweed blooms from May through August, so you are apt to find it no matter when in the summer you visit the coast.

The field chickweed is a widely ranging species that can vary greatly from one area to another. Those found along the coast are usually densely hairy, especially along the upper portion of the plant. Those found in higher mountainous areas are less hairy and tend to have broader leaves than the coastal plants.

Found throughout North America, chickweed is an exotic plant that is often considered to be a weed.

Blue Gilia   *Gilia capitata*

Field Chickweed   *Cerastium arvense*

POPPY FAMILY Papaveraceae

Members of the poppy family found in coastal forests are described
on page 154.

California Poppy *Eschscholtzia californica*

California poppy grows along roadside bluffs and coastal fields. It is
about a foot tall and has finely dissected leaves that are an attractive blue-
green color. The large, showy flowers have four petals, which may be
golden or orange. When the buds first appear, the outer flower parts form
a pointed cap. This is pushed off as the petals unfold. A sun-loving plant,
its flowers close at night. On cloudy days, they may open only partially, or
not at all.

The flowers appear with warm spring weather and may persist throughout the summer, especially where the mild coastal climate allows a second
crop of these colorful annuals from an early seed crop. Because it sprouts
easily from seed, it has been introduced into many places as a garden flower
and is quick to sprout in dry fields and meadows. Early explorers docu-
mented the springtime hillsides covered with this perky wildflower. It is the
beloved state flower of California.

Found in southern Oregon and California. Originally found from the
Columbia River to southern California, it has become established along the
Washington and British Columbia coasts as well.

PRIMROSE FAMILY Primulaceae

A member of the primrose family found in wetlands is described on
page 56.

Pimpernel *Anagallis arvensis*

Pimpernel lies close to the ground, its little, five-petaled, burnt orange
flowers partially hiding amid the leaves. The flower petals are tinged with
purple at the base, making them very attractive. Some individuals have all
purple flowers. The leaves are ovate, sessile, and opposite each other on the
stem.

The genus name *Anagallis* comes from the Greek, meaning "to delight
again," a reference to the way the flowers close at night and reopen during
the day. Because the flower petals roll up during cloudy days, it is also called
"poor man's weather glass."

Originally from Europe and found in most of North America.

California Poppy *Eschscholtzia californica*

Pimpernel *Anagallis arvensis*

PURSLANE FAMILY Portulacaceae

Members of the purslane family found in coastal forests are described on page 156.

Red Maids *Calandrinia ciliata*

Red maids' brilliant red color dots meadows and grassy spots along bluffs and coastal meadows. An annual, it may be either upright or flattened along the ground. The thick, smooth leaves are a glossy green and spread along the stem. They are narrow and linear in shape. The five-petaled flowers close at night, opening at midday. The dainty flowers are about an inch in diameter. Red maids is one of the earliest of coastal flowers to bloom; look for them from February to May. Toward the end of their blooming season, you'll find them in the company of wild hollyhock, thrift, wallflower, and California poppy.

Found from British Columbia to southern California.

ROSE FAMILY Rosaceae

Other members of the rose family are described on pages 24, 58, and 132 to 138. Family characteristics are found on page 132.

Ocean Spray *Holodiscus discolor*

Closely resembling the foam thrown onshore by stiff winds of a coastal storm, ocean spray, also called arrowwood or creambush, is recognizable by its thick plume of tightly clustered white flowers. A shrub 3 to 20 feet tall, it has wedge-shaped, simple leaves. Ocean spray blooms from May through July and is abundant on coastal bluffs, along streams, and in open woods. You'll find it in many of the campgrounds dotting the coast.

Ocean spray is used as an ornamental and graces many northwestern gardens. Indians had a far more important use for it, however. Widely used as shafts for arrows, it was known as "ironwood" by many tribes. The hard wood was also used for canoe paddles, digging sticks, campfire prongs, and many other wooden utensils.

Found from British Columbia south through California and east in the mountains to western Montana.

Red Maids   *Calandrinia ciliata*

Ocean Spray   *Holodiscus discolor*

STONECROP FAMILY   Crassulaceae

The stonecrop family consists of about 1,500 species of herbs and small shrubs with succulent or fleshy leaves and regular (symmetrical) flowers. The family contains many plants that are used widely for garden borders and in rock gardens. Many are cultivated specifically for landscaping. The attractive foliage makes them excellent garden plants year around.

Found on well-drained sites, stonecrops have basal leaves that absorb and store water when it is plentiful. Then, during times of drought, the plant can utilize this stored moisture. This feature is advantageous along the Pacific coast, where summers are often dry and the thin mantle of soil covering rocky headlands holds little moisture.

Live-forever   *Dudleya farinosa*

Also called "hen-and-chickens," these succulent plants dot coastal bluffs and rock outcrops, their basal rosettes looking like gray bouquets on the cliffs. The rosettes are very attractive, a feature that makes other species of this genus popular rock garden plants. The triangular leaves are quite thick and juicy and are covered with a powdery substance, which gives them their pale gray color. The flowering stalk grows about 12 inches above the leaves, each stem carrying smaller succulent leaves scattered along its length. The flower cluster is somewhat flat-topped, with pale yellow or cream-colored flowers.

Found along the California coast to southern Oregon.

Oregon Stonecrop   *Sedum oreganum*

Rocky basalt cliffs along the coast are often splattered with yellow color in early summer. Close inspection reveals the small, star-shaped flowers and rounded, succulent leaves of Oregon stonecrop. Trailing across the rocky nooks with matted, branching rootstocks, this stonecrop has leafy shoots terminated by tight rosettes. The rounded leaves are often tinged with hues of bronze, especially toward the end of the summer. The flowering stems are about 4 inches high. They have bright yellow flowers, each with five petals that are fused at the base.

Found from British Columbia to Oregon.

Broad-leaved Stonecrop   *Sedum spatulifolium*

Broad-leaved stonecrop might easily be confused with Oregon stonecrop. It, too, has star-shaped flowers and succulent leaves; however, its flowers are a pale yellow or cream color and the individual flower petals are completely separate. The leaves are distinctly spatulate (narrow at the base and wider at the tip) in shape, and the basal leaves form conspicuous rosettes. The red-tinged rosettes are attractive additions to coastal rocky bluffs and headlands, even before the flowers appear.

Found from British Columbia to California.

Live-forever *Dudleya farinosa*

Broad-leaved Stonecrop *Sedum spatulifolium*

Oregon Stonecrop *Sedum oreganum*

SUNFLOWER FAMILY   Compositae

The sunflower family is characterized by flowers collected together in dense heads with a common receptacle, giving the appearance of a single flower. The individual flowers are tubular or strap-shaped. Some types are made up entirely of strap (also called ray) flowers; the common dandelion is one example. Others, such as the thistle, have only tubular flowers. Still others contain both types. The sunflower, aster, goldenrod, and daisy are examples of floral heads with both ray and disk flowers.

Members of this family found in other habitats are described on pages 26 to 30, 62, 140, and 158.

Yarrow   *Achillea millefolium*

Yarrow is extremely adaptable. It grows in sandy openings and dunes, along roadsides and in other waste areas, and at timberline in western mountains. It has erect stems 12 to 30 inches tall; however, where it is hit by constant salt spray and coastal winds, it may be much shorter and in small, tufted clumps. The strongly scented leaves are divided into many small segments. The white or pale pink flowers are arranged in heads and consist of two basic types. The center of the head is composed of small tubular flowers. What appear to be individual petals are actually ray- or strap-shaped flowers. There are usually between four or five of these. The entire head looks like a single flower to the novice.

Found throughout North America.

Pearly Everlasting   *Anaphalis margaritacea*

Pearly everlasting is a bunched or loosely tufted plant found in sand dunes and dry openings. It grows 1 to 2 feet tall and has woolly white leaves. The flower heads are in tight, round-topped clusters that expand up to 6 inches across. The flower heads have yellow centers composed of tubular flowers. These flower heads are of two different types: the female, or seed-producing, and the male, or pollen-producing. The flowers are surrounded by overlapping rows of white bracts that are petallike and have the texture of paper. At first glance, these bracts are sometimes thought to be the flower petals. It is the bracts that remain after the other flower parts have withered. They last indefinitely in dried flower arrangements, hence the common name, everlasting. The specific name also means "pearly" and refers to the white color.

When the flowers are young, the central yellow flowers are not very conspicuous. But, as the flower head matures, the white bracts spread and the center flowers enlarge, becoming more visible. The seeds produced are attached to a tuft of fine, straight hairs that act as a parachute and allow the seeds to spread over great distances.

Found in much of North America, Europe, and Asia.

Yarrow *Achillea millefolium*

Yarrow *Achillea millefolium*

Pearly Everlasting *Anaphalis margaritacea*

California Aster
Aster chilensis

California aster begins blooming in late July and August—a few blossoms may still be found in January. Occurring in the grassy areas of coastal campgrounds and roadsides, this aster is quite variable. It grows 1 to 3 feet tall and has long, narrow leaves that clasp the stem. The flower heads have yellow or burnt orange disk flowers and narrow purple ray flowers. The entire head is about an inch across.

Asters generally bloom in the late summer or fall and herald the end of summer. Because they bloom when most other coastal wildflowers have been spent, their blossoms stand out and present a spectacular splash of color in grassy openings.

Found throughout much of the western United States.

English Daisy
Bellis perennis

English daisy is a good example of a plant that is not native to the Northwest, yet has adapted quite well and is now common in areas where it does not have to compete with brushy natural vegetation. Most of the leaves are basal, forming a tidy, little tuft. Each floral head is on its own stem and has yellow disk flowers and ray flowers that range from white to deep pink. English daisy grows 4 to 6 inches tall but, since it is often found in otherwise neatly manicured lawns, English daisy becomes dwarf, continuing to bloom and dotting the green carpet with white. The flowers may be seen through the winter, spring, and summer months, but are most conspicuous during mild coastal winters when other vegetation is dormant. Look for it in coastal parks and waysides, where it often shares the lawns with self-heal flowers and the ubiquitous sea gull.

The genus *Bellis* is a small one, containing only about a half-dozen species. The genus name is derived from the Latin, meaning "pretty," a reference to the small, dainty flower heads.

Found throughout most of the Northwest.

Common Thistle
Cirsium vulgare

Also called bull thistle, the common thistle is a stout plant that grows 2 to 3 feet tall. It has spiny, irregularly lobed leaves that are decurrent, meaning the base of the leaf has small wings that partially clasp the stem. The purple flower heads are quite eye-catching and can be found on open grassy coastal headlands and fields.

Thistles are considered weeds by most observers. This is unfortunate because many of the thistle flower heads, close-up, are quite attractive. It is true, though, that they do invade pastures, fields, roadsides, and areas that have been disturbed and abound in recently logged places.

Many other species of thistle may also be found along the coast. They are difficult to tell apart. Thistles as a group, however, are usually easy to recognize. Their numerous flowers are clustered into a compact head, and they usually have prickly stems and leaves. There may be as many as 200 species of thistle, and many of these are native to North America.

Common thistle is a native of Europe that is found throughout much of North America.

California Aster *Aster chilensis*

Common Thistle *Cirsium vulgare*

English Daisy *Bellis perennis*

Seaside Daisy   *Erigeron glaucus*

Seaside daisy inhabits nooks and crannies in coastal cliffs and banks. Whether its stems are prostrate or erect, they grow from creeping rhizomes and a stout root, sometimes forming a low-growing mat. The thick leaves are mostly basal, although a few are also scattered along the 2- to 12-inch-tall flowering stem. There are from one to six flowering heads on each stem: the central disk flowers range from burnt orange to yellow, while the ray flowers range from pink or lavender to almost white. Where the ocean winds and salt spray are severe, the entire plant may be dwarf-sized, except for the flower heads, which are always 1 to 2 inches across. Seaside daisy is never out of sight of the sea and blooms from June through August.

In some areas of the coast, seaside daisy has become a popular garden plant. The tufted form of the plant and its large flowers make it a good garden addition. It can be started either from seed or from cuttings. Seed germinates quickly in sandy soil and can be started either in flats and later transferred or can be sown directly on open ground. During the dry coastal summer, seaside daisy normally thrives on little moisture except for fog. Light watering should assure a long blooming period in the garden.

Found along the coasts of Oregon and California.

Woolly Sunflower   *Eriophyllum lanatum*

Also called golden yarrow, the genus *Eriophyllum* is a variable one, ranging widely over the western states. At higher elevations, it may be quite short in stature; in moist lowlands along the western slopes of the Cascade-Sierra range, it may be bushy in shape. Along the coast it may appear stunted, due perhaps to the wind and salt spray. Nonetheless, it is quite distinctive. The bright yellow flower heads have both ray and disk flowers. The stems bear leaves that are entire or deeply cleft, but always covered with woolly white hairs that give them a gray shade. The stems emerge from a woody base and may grow up to 2 feet tall.

Woolly sunflower is a welcome addition to a wildflower rock garden. The woolly leaves makes it an attractive plant, even when it is not flowering. The scientific name *Eriophyllum* means "woolly foliage."

Found throughout much of the northwestern states.

Gold Fields   *Lasthenia macrantha*

Contrasting with the blue of the ocean, gold fields blankets coastal meadows with mats of gold. You'll find it in sunny, sandy spots, blooming from early spring through much of the summer. The large yellow flowers seem to make the rest of the slender plant top-heavy and almost hide the matted leaves below. The stems are erect or spreading, with linear, opposite leaves. The inch-wide, floral heads have both ray and disk flowers. Intermingled with the grasses of coastal bluffs, gold fields usually grows only 6 to 12 inches tall.

Found from the central California coast north into Oregon.

Seaside Daisy *Erigeron glaucus*

Woolly Sunflower *Eriophyllum lanatum*

Gold Fields *Lasthenia macrantha*

Tidy Tips   *Layia platyglossa*

This cheery little plant carpets hillsides and grassy slopes with its bright flowers. Each flower head sits atop its own stem. The 1½-inch-wide flower head has yellow petallike ray flowers with a white outer band. The central disk flowers are also sunshine yellow. The flowers bloom from March through May. Tidy tips fills the air with its sweet fragrance and is one of the wildflowers that contributes to the golden colors of springtime along the California coast and in the mountain foothills.

Found throughout much of California.

Common Daisy   *Leucanthemum vulgare*

Everyone recognizes the common daisy, which is also known as marguerite and ox-eye daisy. This is the flower used to make daisy chains and the flower made famous by the chant "loves me, loves me not." Growing 1 to 2 feet tall, each of a daisy's flower heads sits on its own long stem and is about 2 inches across. The disk flowers are yellow while the ray flowers are white. Alternate leaves are scattered along the stem, and are pinnately lobed or parted. Common daisy adorns grassy hillsides and open fields with gay flowers that bloom through most of the summer.

A native of Europe, the common daisy is another example of a plant that reached North American shores with early settlers, either accidentally, with seeds mixed in household goods or food items, or purposely as garden stock.

Found throughout much of North America.

Tansy Ragwort   *Senecio jacobaea*

Tansy ragwort, adorned with clusters of yellow flower heads, may be found in open areas, along roadsides, in pastures, and along sandy spits and river edges. It lends a golden hue to grassy headlands in July and August. Growing from 1 to 6 feet tall, tansy ragwort has stout stems and leaves that are divided into lobed and toothed segments. The golden flowering heads are quite numerous: each flower head has ten to fifteen ray flowers surrounding the disk flowers. This makes a clump of them quite showy and colorful, wherever they happen to grow.

During the first year that a tansy ragwort sprouts, clumps of dark green leaves appear. The following year, the stems grow, branch freely, and produce the colorful flowers for which tansy is known. It has the ability to sprout anew from bits of root that have been cut. These traits make it a very aggressive weed. Since it is toxic, it is not welcome in fields and pastures.

A native of Europe, tansy ragwort first became established in the northeastern states and has spread aggressively.

Found in much of North America.

Tidy Tips   *Layia platyglossa*

Common Daisy   *Leucanthemum vulgare*

Tansy Ragwort   *Senecio jacobaea*

109

Canada Goldenrod   *Solidago canadensis*

Goldenrod flaunts its colorful plumes of flowers during August and September. It is particularly spectacular along the bluffs overlooking the ocean. Growing from creeping underground stems, a clump of goldenrod resembles a small shrub or bush, and may reach 6 feet in height (although most are 2 to 3 feet tall). The entire stem is leafy, the leaves being lance-shaped and toothed along the edge. The small, yellow flower heads are in thick terminal plumes. Quite common along the coast, this goldenrod grows equally well in fields, meadow edges, and roadsides.

Found throughout much of North America.

VIOLET FAMILY   Violaceae

Additional violets are described on page 160.

Western Blue Violet   *Viola adunca*

This violet has several tufted stems with heart-shaped leaves. The flower stems are a little longer than the leaves. The flowers themselves closely resemble those of the garden violet. Its deep blue or purple flowers have the characteristic violet floral pattern of five petals of unequal size. The lower petal is often larger than the other four and is variously shaped. In this violet, it is a long, slender spur.

Found in much of the Pacific Northwest.

Canada Goldenrod   *Solidago canadensis*

Western Blue Violet   *Viola adunca*

Western Blue Violet   *Viola adunca*

Brushfields

Brushfields form the transition between open grasslands and a forest cover. Shrubs and young trees gradually invade openings such as grassy meadows, pastures, or partially stabilized dunes. On the coast they are usually very colorful, being made up of some of North America's most spectacular flowering shrubs; the azalea, rhododendron, pink-flowering currant, and elderberry are examples. In addition, several exotic species, noticeably gorse and Scotch broom, have invaded many coastal areas, often competing with native species.

The mild coastal climate encourages luxuriant growth, and often these brushlands are nearly impossible to walk through. They thus serve the very important function of providing a dense cover that protects steep slopes from erosion and offers shelter for various forms of wildlife. The coasts of southern Oregon and northern California differ somewhat from those farther north. The shrub and forest communities seen along the northern Pacific coast are replaced farther south by communities of herbs and low shrubs, allowing grass-covered slopes and brushfields to dominate. Probably, the warmer, drier climate of this stretch of shoreline has much to do with this change. The greater frequency of fog and the predominance of high bluffs and steep slopes immediately adjacent to the ocean may be other factors.

BUCKTHORN FAMILY Rhamnaceae

Blue Blossom *Ceanothus thysiflorus*

During the early part of the summer, blue blossom spreads its hue over the coastal brushfields of southern Oregon, the redwood region of northern California, and central California. A shrub, or small tree, between 3 and 20 feet tall, its small flowers are in showy, round-topped clusters at the end of the branches. As is typical of other members of this group, the fragrant flowers have five petals that are hooded and long-clawed, somewhat resembling a spoon. The stamens extend beyond the other flower parts, producing a fuzzy appearance. The alternate leaves have three prominent veins and are 1 to 2 inches long.

Found from southern Oregon through central California.

Another *Ceanothus* is described on page 68.

CURRANT FAMILY Grossulariaceae

Pink-flowering Currant *Ribes sanguineum*

This brightly colored shrub, which blooms in March and April, is a harbinger of spring. It is one of the earliest of our coastal shrubs to bloom. The pale pink to deep rose-colored flowers are only ¼ to ½ inch long; however, since they are in pendant clusters about 4 inches long, the mass is quite conspicuous. The leaves are club-shaped, with three to five lobes. Pink-flowering currant is a shrub 3 to 12 feet tall. It grows along forest borders and in old logged areas (where it is often found growing on an old stump), as well as on partially reforested dune areas.

Found from British Columbia to central California.

Similar plant: **Prickly gooseberry** (*Ribes menziesii*) could be confused with pink-flowering currant. It can be found along the coast of California and southern Oregon. It is an upright shrub, 3 to 6 feet tall, with forked spines along the stem. Smaller bristles occur on the young shoots. The hairy leaves are 1 to 2 inches wide and divided into three to five lobes. Dark red or purple flowers occur singly or in pairs; these are replaced later in the year by purple berries, which are covered with fine bristles.

Blue Blossom *Ceanothus thysiflorus*

Blue Blossom *Ceanothus thysiflorus*

Pink-flowering Currant *Ribes sanguineum*

EVENING PRIMROSE FAMILY   Onagraceae

Other members of this family are described on pages 12 and 72.

Fireweed   *Epilobium angustifolium*

Fireweed colors abandoned fields, forest openings, and burned areas (which accounts for the common name). Another common name is willow herb, because of the resemblance of the leaves to those of the willow.

Fireweed grows up to 7 feet tall, with spear-shaped leaves along the entire length. The plume of pink or red flowers, however, is fireweed's most distinctive feature. They begin to bloom in early summer, the flower cluster blooming from the bottom upward. The flowers are followed by thin seed pods, or capsules, that split linearly into four parts when ripe, expelling the seeds. Each seed carries a feathery plume that aids its dispersion. Fireweed spreads not only by seeds but also by buds on the underground stem.

Fireweed has long been used by inhabitants of the northern areas of Europe and North America for food. The young shoots are cut and eaten like asparagus. It is also well known for its nectar. Beekeepers regularly seek out prime fireweed areas for the production of premium honey. Few coastal Indians, however, are known to have used fireweed as a food supply. Perhaps, because of the lack of openings in the dense timber, there were not enough sunny, brushy spots to encourage fireweed growth.

Found from Alaska south through California and east across northern North America. Also found in northern Europe and Asia.

HEATH FAMILY   Ericaceae

This large family contains mostly small trees, or shrubs, and perennial herbs. The flowers are generally bell-shaped, with the flower parts in fives or fours. Many plants have leathery or evergreen leaves. Familiar examples include the wintergreen, huckleberry, rhododendron, azalea, and cranberry.

Wetlands members of this family are described on page 46.

Madrone   *Arbutus menziesii*

This evergreen, broad-leaved tree is one of the most beautiful plants on the Pacific coast. Resembling an overgrown manzanita (a close relative), madrone grows to 90 feet tall, has shiny red bark, pendant clusters of white, urn-shaped flowers, and bright scarlet berries. Madrone blooms along U.S. Highway 101 in April and May, making a spectacular spring display.

Indians and early settlers both had many uses for madrone. The root, bark, and leaves were steeped in water to make a brew for colds. The bark, which rolls off each year, was used to make a tea for soothing stomachaches. The hard wood was used as support for Indian dwellings and for the making of many small tools, such as digging sticks.

The first botanist to note the madrone was Archibald Menzies, who sailed to the Pacific coast with the Vancouver Expedition of 1790. This intrepid traveler was the first white man to see many of the Northwest's most conspicuous plants, including the Douglas fir and the redwood.

Found from British Columbia to Baja California.

Fireweed *Epilobium angustifolium*

Madrone *Arbutus menziesii*

Manzanita
Arctostaphylos species

Manzanitas are shrubs with leathery, evergreen leaves and smooth, polished bark. The older, outer bark peels, revealing the dark red or bronze of the new bark. The pink or white flowers are urn-shaped and usually hang in small clusters.

Manzanita fruits, especially those of the larger species, resemble little apples. In fact, the word *manzanita* is Spanish, meaning "little apple." This genus contains some fifty species, mostly in California. Many species are quite large and bushy. The Indians made a drink much like cider from the fruits. In some areas the gathering of manzanita fruit was combined with great feasting. The hard wood of the larger species was used for making various types of tools, such as digging sticks.

Hairy Manzanita
Arctostaphylos columbiana

Hairy manzanita is a brushy shrub 2 to 8 feet tall. The compact clusters of flowers are pale pink or white and bloom in late April or May. The young twigs are densely covered with bristly hairs. Hairy manzanita grows best in rocky soil and partially vegetated dune areas. Because of its hardiness and ability to grow in sterile situations, it is often used for roadside landscaping.

Found from British Columbia through northern California.

Kinnikinnick
Arctostaphylos uva-ursi

Also called bearberry, kinnikinnick is a prostrate plant, rarely growing more than 6 inches in height. Its creeping nature sometimes allows it to cover large areas of sand or dry banks. It has shiny green, leathery-textured leaves. The pink lanternlike flowers are quite fragrant and transform into small scarlet berries by the end of the summer.

In the Northwest, kinnikinnick leaves were primarily used by American Indians and, later, by trappers and traders, as a smoking mixture. The leaves were made into a powder and smoked alone until the introduction of tobacco by white trappers and settlers. Then, kinnikinnick leaves were mixed with tobacco.

Today, kinnikinnick is widely used for landscaping roadways and banks, where its sturdy stems and leaves help prevent erosion. It is quite hardy and tolerates both hot sun and freezing temperatures. Usually started by layering, new plants grow slowly. Once established, however, they make a fine garden border and are often planted along retaining walls, where the shiny stems hang gracefully over the edge. State highway officials are learning the advantages of using maintenance-free native plants such as kinnikinnick on road shoulders and in parks.

Found across northern North America, south along the coasts and in the mountains. Also found in northern Europe and Asia.

118

Hairy Manzanita
Arctostaphylos columbiana

Kinnikinnick
Arctostaphylos uva-ursi

Kinnikinnick   *Arctostaphylos uva-ursi*

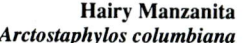

Salal   *Gaultheria shallon*

Salal is well known to most residents of the Pacific Northwest. It can be barely 6 inches tall or a robust bush of 5 feet or more. It attains its most luxuriant growth along the forest borders and brushfields of the Pacific coast, where the wind often prunes it into a thick, impenetrable hedge. The evergreen leaves are thick and leathery and 3 to 4 inches long. Urn-shaped flowers bloom from May through July and become juicy blue-black berries.

Coastal Indians used the salal berries as a basic food item that could be prepared in a variety of ways. The most common method of preparation was to mash the berries so that they could be dried and made into small cakes. Later, these cakes were dipped in whale oil or seal oil and eaten. They were also eaten fresh. Sometimes the salal was dried in large quantities and shaped into large loaves resembling bread. Early settlers learned to make a syrup and pies from the salal berry; it also makes an excellent jam or jelly.

Salal was one of David Douglas's favorite North American plants. (See page 94 for information about Douglas.) He introduced salal into Europe, where it has been used as a garden plant. Only recently has it come into its own for landscaping in the Northwest. Its large evergreen leaves make an excellent ground cover.

Found from British Columbia to southern California.

Salal *Gaultheria shallon*

Salal bearing fruit *Gaultheria shallon*

RHODODENDRON *Rhododendron* species

The *Rhododendron* group consists of small shrubs with alternate leaves and showy, somewhat bell-shaped flowers. The word *rhododendron* comes from the Greek for "rose tree," attesting to the renowned beauty of the genus in ancient times.

Pacific Rhododendron *Rhododendron macrophyllum*

A visit to the Pacific coast in May or June is a color treat. The fresh green of spring blends with the deep purple or rosered of the Pacific rhododendron. An evergreen shrub, 5 to 10 feet tall, it attains a neat, compact form when in the open, but more often is a straggling, sparsely branched shrub when it is part of the forest understory. The blossoms form clusters 6 inches or more across and are especially spectacular against the green background of the forest edge. The leathery, oblong leaves have slightly rolled-under edges.

Today, the Pacific rhododendron is widely acclaimed as one of the most beautiful of our native shrubs. It has been declared the state flower of Washington, and several coastal communities have festivals to commemorate the time of blooming. Many horticultural varieties have been developed and grace lawns and gardens. Although the native rhododendron is generally a pale pink or rose color, commercial nurseries now offer shrubs with flowers ranging from white and yellow to deep purple.

Found from British Columbia to northern California.

Western Azalea *Rhododendron occidentale*

A spectacular shrub of coastal brushfields when it blooms in late April and May, azalea often forms dense thickets. When pruned and battered by coastal winds, the shrubs grow only 2 to 3 feet high; farther inland, where they grow in more sheltered spots, the graceful shrubs reach 14 feet in height. The fragrant, funnel-shaped flowers are 1 to 2 inches long. They are pink or white and have a large yellow blotch on the inner part of the upper lobe. The five stamens extend beyond the flower tube, adding to the beauty of the flower.

Many local communities celebrate "azalea days" to herald the coming summer. An especially beautiful azalea display may be seen along the old coastal highway north of Gold Beach, Oregon.

Found from southern Oregon to central California along the coast, and also in the Sierra Nevada.

Pacific Rhododendron   *Rhododendron macrophyllum*

Western Azalea   *Rhododendron occidentale*

HUCKLEBERRY   *Vaccinium* species
Several species of huckleberry are found in the Northwest. They are usually small shrubs with alternate leaves and have small hanging flowers that are bell-shaped or urn-shaped. The tasty berries are dark blue or red. They are frequently understory shrubs in open forests or, more commonly, occur along forest borders and open brushfields.

Evergreen Huckleberry   *Vaccinium ovatum*
An evergreen shrub, this huckleberry has shiny, leathery, and oblong or ovate leaves with toothed edges. The bell-shaped flowers are pale pink and grow in small clusters that hang from the axils of the leaves. The tasty black berries that appear at the end of the summer are eagerly gathered by coastal residents and travelers alike. The attractive shrubs are common in the well-kept campgrounds of Olympic National Park and Oregon Dunes National Recreation Area. Campers along the coast regularly visit their favorite campground to pick ripe huckleberries, which can be made into jams, jellies, pies, and syrups. This huckleberry also makes a good landscaping plant. The shiny leaves are evergreen, making them attractive year-round.
Found from British Columbia to northern California.

Red Huckleberry   *Vaccinium parvifolium*
Red huckleberry is found in dense woodlands, partial shade, or in open brushfields. It is characterized by pale, urn-shaped flowers, thin, green leaves, bright red berries, and stems that are distinctly angled. The berries are much sparser in this species, and therefore more difficult to gather. This huckleberry is often seen growing from the stumps remaining in areas that have been burned or otherwise disturbed.
Found from British Columbia to central California.

Evergreen Huckleberry *Vaccinium ovatum*

Red Huckleberry fruits *Vaccinium parvifolium*

Red Huckleberry in flower *Vaccinium parvifolium*

HONEYSUCKLE FAMILY Caprifoliaceae

A member of the honeysuckle family found in wetlands is described on page 46.

Elderberry *Sambucus racemosa*

Elderberry grows in moist forest edges, open brushy slopes, and sunny coastal campgrounds. A small tree, or shrub, growing 5 to 20 feet tall, red elderberry is recognized in the spring and early summer by its flat to pyramidal cluster of white flowers and compound leaves of five leaflets. Red elderberry acquires its common name, however, because of its bright red fruit. The clusters of red berries attract as much attention as the flower plumes, making it an attractive shrub in coastal areas nearly all summer. These berries are eaten by a wide variety of animals. Flocks of band-tailed pigeons, for instance, feast on them, often completely consuming the crop.

Found from southern Alaska to California.

Similar plant: This elderberry could possibly be confused with the **blue elderberry** (*Sambucus cerulea*), which is often found in coastal valleys. The cluster of white flowers is flat, never dome-shaped. When the pale blue fruits appear, however, there can be no mistake.

Elderberry　*Sambucus racemosa*

Blue Elderberry　*Sambucus cerulea*

Elderberry fruit　*Sambucus racemosa*

LILY FAMILY Liliaceae

Other members of the lily family are described on pages 48, 82, and
148 to 152.

Tiger Lily *Lilium columbianum*

Also called Columbia lily, tiger lily is occasionally found on brushy
hillsides in the company of chaparral broom and blackberries. You'll
recognize this spectacular lily by its nodding flowers with backward
curving petals and by its whorled leaves. These are mounted along a 1- to
3-foot-tall stem, although specimens of 5 to 6 feet tall are sometimes found.
A great deal of variation occurs in this lily. Flowers may occur singly, or a
plant may bear many blossoms. The flower color ranges from pale orange
to almost yellow to deep burnt orange. Dark purple spots decorate the petals.

Found from British Columbia to northern California.

Tiger Lily   *Lilium columbianum*

PEA FAMILY   Leguminaceae

Members of the pea family found on coastal beaches and dunes are described on pages 18 to 20; those found in wetlands are described on page 54.

Scotch Broom   *Cytisus scoparius*

These gaily flowered shrubs stand out along the Pacific coast, especially when at the peak of flowering in May. The golden flowers color dry slopes, road shoulders, bluffs, and dune areas, where Scotch broom has been planted in the past for sand stabilization. Although most flowers are pure yellow, occasionally they are spotted with purple or maroon. This shrub grows up to 9 feet tall and has small, three-parted leaves and angled, green stems. The brightly colored flowers appear singly, usually in the axils of the leaves. They are replaced by dark, hairy pods, which pop open when ripe, scattering seeds in every direction. On a warm still day, you can hear the crackling, popping sound.

Scotch broom is an introduced plant. Seeds from the British consulate in the Sandwich Islands, as Hawaii was then called, were planted near Victoria, British Columbia, in the 1850s. Although only a few of them grew, it was enough to establish this aggressive shrub on the Northwest coast.

Found along the Northwest coast.

Similar plant: **French broom** (*Genista monspessulanus*) has yellow, pea-shaped flowers and is very similar in appearance to Scotch broom. However, its yellow flowers are borne in clusters of three to ten, while those of Scotch broom are single. The flowers are also a paler yellow color than those of Scotch broom.

French broom is a native of the Canary Islands. It was introduced as a garden plant in western Washington, western Oregon, and northern California, but escaped cultivation.

Found locally along the Northwest coast, from British Columbia to southern California.

Gorse   *Ulex europaea*

Gorse is sometimes confused with the brooms. Like them, it is covered by golden, pea-shaped flowers in the spring. But it is also densely covered with green spines, which makes it easy to distinguish and very difficult to walk through. Gorse begins blooming in January along the California coast and reaches the peak of color in late spring. Many people admire its brightly colored flowers; it makes an attractive hedgerow. Unfortunately, it has a high oil content and is therefore very flammable. Its ability to burn explosively was largely responsible for the 1936 fire that partially destroyed the town of Bandon on the southern Oregon coast.

Introduced from Europe as an ornamental in the late 1800s, it has spread rapidly. Many of the large, aggressive flowering shrubs of our Pacific coast are exotics. These include broom, gorse, and tree lupine. In many cases, these introduced plants adapt well to the mild Pacific climate and soon dominate an area, crowding out native species.

Found in much of the western portions of the Pacific Northwest, especially along the coast.

Scotch Broom *Cytisus scoparius*

French Broom *Genista monspessulanus*

Gorse *Ulex europaea*

131

ROSE FAMILY
Rosaceae

The rose family contains a wide variety of plants, including trees, shrubs, and herbs. The flowers generally have five petals, which are usually attached with the other floral parts to a saucer- or cup-shaped base. This family supplies important fruit crops, such as strawberry, raspberry, loganberry, apple, and cherry. In addition, many species have been cultivated for their beautiful flowers. Examples include the rose, spirea, and potentilla.

Other members of this family are discussed on pages 24, 58, and 98.

Goat's Beard
Aruncus dioicus

A 3- to 6-foot-tall plant, goat's beard, also known as sea foam, is best known for its plumes of white flowers. Arranged in narrow pencillike groups, the flower clusters make a showy display in May and June. The narrow plumes of flowers slowly wither into brownish strings of seed, which persist through part of the winter and aid its identification. Goat's beard is commonly found along shady forest borders.

At first glance, goat's beard appears to be a shrub because of its large size; however, since it dies back each winter and has no woody tissue, it is actually an herb. It grows rapidly each spring from an underground stem.

Found throughout much of North America. A cosmopolitan plant, it also occurs in Europe and Asia.

Goat's Beard *Aruncus dioicus*

Indian Plum   *Oemleria cerasiformis*

Before any of the coastal brushfields have begun to leaf out, the pendant white flowers of Indian plum, also called osoberry or arrowwood, begin to bloom. The leaves first appear in small bunches, making them stand out against their drab background. Indian plum is a shrub, or small tree, 4 to 9 feet tall, which grows best in the companionship of other shrubby species, such as alder and willow. Look for it in brushfields, forest borders, and along roadsides.

After the flowers are spent, Indian plum blends into the other greenery. A small berry or "plum" develops by midsummer. A bluish purple color, it is quite bitter. Although most coastal Indians ate these plums, they did not regard them as an important part of their diet, probably because of the bitter taste. Robins, cedar waxwings, and other birds, however, eat them with relish, often stripping a small shrub of its fruit in only a few hours. Some reference guides list this shrub as a source of straight wood for arrows, hence the name arrowwood.

Found from British Columbia to California.

Wild Rose   *Rosa nutkana*

The wild rose is one of the favorites of all wildflowers. Four states (Georgia, Iowa, New York, and North Dakota) have selected a wild rose as their state flower. Usually the wild rose is easily identified as a rose; however, individual species often hybridize and are difficult to tell apart. Wild roses are prickly shrubs with alternate, pinnately compound leaves (meaning the leaflets are arranged along a common shaft, as with a feather). Wild roses may be erect, climbing, or trailing along the ground. The flowers usually have five pink petals. The fleshy round fruits are called hips and are rich in vitamin C.

Common wild rose is one of the most showy of our native roses, largely because of its deep pink flowers, which may be 2 inches across. It is most often found in moist, wooded areas. Look for this rose blooming along coastal highways in mid-May and June.

Many coastal Indians used rose hips for food, some combining them with dried salmon eggs. The peeled twigs and leaves were also boiled and used as a hot beverage. Dried rose hips can be purchased in many health food stores for use in making tea.

Found from Alaska to northern California.

Indian Plum   *Oemleria cerasiformis*

Wild Rose   *Rosa nutkana*

BLACKBERRY   *Rubus* species

The *Rubus* group contains shrubs, which may be trailing or erect, and often have prickles or thorns. The flowers have five petals and numerous stamens. The fruits are made up of an aggregate of many small fleshy fruits, usually arranged in a thimble shape. The raspberry and blackberry are typical.

Himalayan Blackberry   *Rubus discolor*

Blackberries grow wild on the west side of the Cascade-Sierra divide, brushing over hedgerows, roadside borders, meadows, and other waste areas. They are either a blessing or a curse, depending on whether you wish to pick the berries or attempt to travel through them. Many species of wild blackberries can be found along the Pacific coast; Himalayan blackberry is perhaps the best known, both because of its stout size and its large, tasty berries, which regularly are picked for pies, jam, jelly, and wine. It has large bristles that curve backward, palmately compound leaves, and thick erect or climbing stems. An introduced species, it is considered a pest by farmers who must eradicate it from their fields.

Found from British Columbia south into California and east to Idaho.

Similar plant: **Evergreen bramble** (*Rubus laciniatus*) is also fairly common along the coast. Its leaves, however, are evergreen, and the leaflets are deeply lobed. Himalayan blackberry has leaflets that are merely toothed, and, although a few leaves may persist through the winter, they are not evergreen.

Himalayan Blackberry   *Rubus discolor*

Thimbleberry

Rubus parviflorus

Thimbleberry is a common shrub of the coastal zone. It has large, broadly lobed, maplelike leaves with short hairs that give them a velvety texture. A shrub growing 3 to 6 feet high, its stems lack thorns or prickles. The flowers are white, and each of the five petals has a crinkled texture. The red berries that ripen at the end of summer are like soft raspberries and are responsible for the name, thimbleberry. To some, the flavor is rather bland; nonetheless, they make a welcome snack while hiking.

Found throughout the western states as far east as the Great Lakes area.

Salmonberry

Rubus spectabilis

Salmonberry is quite common along roadsides and brushfields. It is a shrub, growing 3 to 12 feet tall, and is responsible for the dense, shrubby growth along much of U.S. 101. Its tangled mass impedes hikers and cross-country travelers. It has leaves divided into three coarsely toothed leaflets, small thorns on its stems, and five-petaled rose-colored flowers that are about an inch wide. These flowers bloom in April and May, sometimes hanging partially hidden beneath the leaves. Often, scattered blossoms will be found throughout the summer months. The berries, which somewhat resemble raspberries, come in two colors: a clear orange and a deeper red. Both provide good munching, but the clear orange berry is usually considered the most tasty.

Found throughout much of the Pacific Northwest.

Thimbleberry *Rubus parviflorus*

Salmonberry *Rubus spectabilis*

SILK TASSEL FAMILY Garryaceae

Silk Tassel *Garrya elliptica*

The silk tassel is aptly named. Its silvery tassels of flowers gracefully hang from the evergreen shrubs, which grow 3 to 15 feet tall and have wavy-edged leaves. Blooming in the winter or early spring, the pendant flowers become globose fruits only on some of the trees. The male, or pollen-bearing, flowers with their slender, hanging anthers occur on different plants from the female, or seed-bearing, flowers. Only the female shrubs develop fruit. Silk tassel is fairly common on brushy slopes and hills overlooking the ocean.

Found from central Oregon along the coast to California.

Similar plant: **Bearbrush** (*Garrya fremontii*) has smooth-edged leaves. It grows both along the coast and in the coast range and inland valleys of southern Oregon and northern California.

SUNFLOWER FAMILY Compositae

Other members of the sunflower family are described on pages 26 to 30, 62, 102 to 110, and 158.

Chaparral Broom *Baccharis pilularis*

Also known as coyote bush, chaparral broom blooms in the fall on bluffs and banks along the coast. It is a many-branched shrub, growing 2 to 5 feet tall, with alternate, irregularly toothed, leathery leaves and cream-colored flowers in small clusters. Like the flowers of the silk tassel, the seed-bearing flowers are found on different plants from the pollen-bearing flowers. By January or February, the female flowers have become silky puffs of seed heads that fill the air. Because it blooms when most other plants have become dormant, chaparral broom is quite conspicuous. It is also noticeable because its leaves are evergreen, making them stand out against the subdued browns and golds of autumn.

Found along the Oregon and California coasts.

Lizard Tail *Eriophyllum staechadifolium*

This shrubby plant, also called golden yarrow or seaside woolly sun-flower, grows 1 to 3 feet tall. Lizard tail is characterized by yellow flower heads and narrow leaves that have a dense, woolly covering of hairs that make them feel like felt. In open areas, the shrubs are pruned by the coastal winds and may form a dense mat. The yellow flower heads bloom from April through September.

Found along the central California coast.

Silk Tassel *Garrya elliptica*

Chaparral Broom *Baccharis pilularis*

Lizard Tail *Eriophyllum staechadifolium*

Coastal Forests

Forests of pine, spruce, Douglas fir, and hemlock dominate the bluffs along the ocean in northern Oregon, Washington, and British Columbia. These forests include a thick, many-layered understory of shrubs and shade-loving herbs. Grassy openings, especially on south-facing slopes, increase in frequency in southern Oregon and northern California.

There is a natural succession from brushfields to forests. Shrubs and bushy plants, along with young trees, gradually invade openings and coastal prairies. The trees eventually grow above the shrubs, producing a dense canopy that filters out the sunlight. Plants that are shade-tolerant, meaning they can grow in deep shade, manage to grow on the cool forest floor and often produce a continuous mat. It is here that you will find trillium, bleedingheart, sorrel, miner's lettuce, wild ginger, and violet. Some of the shrubs of the brushfield persist as part of the understory, but they are usually less bushy and have fewer stems.

Coastal forests are chiefly comprised of several conifer species: shore pine (*Pinus contorta*), sitka spruce (*Picea sitchensis*), Douglas fir (*Pseudotsuga menziesii*), western hemlock (*Tsuga heterophylla*), coastal redwood (*Sequoia sempervirens*), and Bishop pine (*Pinus muricata*). The shore pine is found just above the high-tide line and endures the full effect of wind and salt spray. It can grow in mineral soil and may, when young, form dense thickets in interdunal swales. Sitka spruce is strictly a fog-belt species and grows only in close proximity to the coast. It can form a dense forest, excluding other species. Because it grows on coastal bluffs, it is often shaped and gnarled by the salt spray and wind. Western hemlock and Douglas fir are not typically shore trees, but are the dominant species of the lowland forests of the coast range. Where sand dunes migrate inland, they often bury western hemlock and Douglas fir. The redwood forms a unique forest, growing best in a very narrow band along the coast, but it is less prevalent on ocean-facing slopes because it does not tolerate salt spray. Bishop pine forms open forests along the central California coastal slopes.

BIRTHWORT FAMILY

Aristolochiaceae

Wild Ginger

Asarum caudatum

Growing freely through the leaf mold of damp coastal woodlands, the heart-shaped leaves of wild ginger are easily recognized both by their shape and their velvety-textured surface. The dark rose-colored flowers are hidden beneath the leaves and hug the ground. The flowers are cup-shaped with three lobes, each of which has a long, tapering tip. The sprawling wild ginger rarely grows more than a few inches tall and blooms during the spring and early summer along the coast.

The scaly rootstocks of *Asarum* are quite fragrant, emitting the scent of ginger. While these rootstocks have been used as a seasoning in natural food recipes, they are too mild to be used commercially.

Found from British Columbia to northern California and inland through Idaho.

BROOM-RAPE FAMILY

Orobanchaceae

Ground Cone

Boschniakia hookeri

It takes a sharp eye to spot ground cone. Resembling a stout, oversized fir cone squatting on the forest floor, ground cone is well named. The fleshy stems are 3 to 6 inches tall, and the entire plant is purple or, sometimes, pale yellow. The leaves are merely overlapping bracts that partially conceal the flowers, which are sessile and attach directly to the stout little stem.

Ground cone is a fairly host-specific parasite, deriving its nourishment from the roots of chlorophyll-bearing (green) plants; it is most often associated with salal. You'll find ground cone in May and June in the sandy soil of dunes that have been covered with a coastal forest of spruce, huckleberry, and salal.

Found from Vancouver Island to central California.

Similar plant: In southern Oregon and in California another ground cone is found: **California ground cone** (*Boschniakia strobilacea*). Its bracts are widest at their upper end while those of *Boschniakia hookeri* are widest across the middle.

Wild Ginger   *Asarum caudatum*

Ground Cone   *Boschniakia hookeri*

FIGWORT FAMILY Scrophulariaceae

Other members of the figwort family are described on pages 42 and 74 to 76.

Spring Queen *Synthyris reniformis*

One of our earliest blooming wildflowers, spring queen, also called grouse flower or snow queen, begins unfolding its dainty blue flowers in mid-February. Although occasionally found on partially sunny banks, it is most often found on a mossy bed in shaded areas. It grows 2 to 8 inches tall, with basal leaves that are kidney- or heart-shaped. The leaves partially cover the delicate flowers, which are in small clusters of six to eight. Look closely at the individual flowers: two purple-tipped stamens protrude from the basket that is formed by four pale purple or blue petals. Because of spring queen's small size, it is often necessary to get down on hands and knees and part the fallen leaves and clumps of moss under which it grows to see these delightful little flowers.

The name spring queen comes from the early blooming date of the flowers. Although a lowly plant in stature, its early arrival during the spring makes it the queen of the forest. The name grouse flower comes from its association with the mating time of the sooty or blue grouse. The soft hooting sounds of the grouse may be heard in the woods at the same time this flower is blooming.

Found in western Oregon and Washington.

Spring Queen *Synthyris reniformis*

LILY FAMILY Liliaceae

The lily family is a large and very important family of plants. Most members of the family grow from bulbs or bulblike structures known as rhizomes. The flowers are often very showy, and the flower parts are in threes. Onions, lilies, yuccas, asparagus, and tulips are examples.

Other members of the lily family are described on pages 48, 82, and 128.

Red Clintonia *Clintonia andrewsiana*

The bright red flowers of clintonia nod at travelers along the shaded roadways of Redwoods National Park. The clusters of flowers top a 2-foot-tall, leafless stem and are replaced by shiny blue berries by midsummer. The leaves are also conspicuous. They are 10 to 12 inches long and flattened against the brown duff of the forest floor.

Found from central California to southwestern Oregon.

Fairy Lanterns *Disporum smithii*

This dainty lily graces coastal woodlands; look for it in the dense shade of Olympic Peninsula forests and in the redwoods. The hanging flowers resemble small lanterns and are cream-colored or white. They are in clusters of two or three at the end of the leafy stems. The leaves clasp the stem, almost giving the stem the appearance of being threaded through the edge of each leaf. The fruits that replace the flowers are bright orange or red berries.

Found from British Columbia to California.

Similar species: **Fairy bells** (*Disporum hookeri*) looks much the same, except the floral petals flare outward. In fairy lanterns they hang down.

Red Clintonia
Clintonia andrewsiana

Red Clintonia
Clintonia andrewsiana

Fairy Lanterns *Disporum smithii*

False Lily-of-the-valley   *Maianthemum dilatatum*

Carpets of this little lily, also known as may-lily, deerberry, and beadruby, cover the ground beneath the dense shade of coastal forests. The plant spreads easily by underground stems, allowing it to cover large areas. The shiny green, heart-shaped leaves are attractive all summer long. As they emerge from the soil in the early spring, they are rolled into an oblong sheath. In May and June, the 12-inch-tall stems bearing white flowers appear. The flowers are tightly clustered at the upper portion of the stem, creating a linear tassel of white. Red berries replace the flowers later in the summer.

Found from Alaska to northern California.

False Solomon's Seal   *Smilacina racemosa*

A plume of small white flowers at the end of an unbranched stem distinguishes false Solomon's seal. Growing between 1 and 3 feet tall from a creeping underground stem, false Solomon's seal is common in shaded conifer forests. The flowers bloom from April through June along the Pacific coast. By the end of the summer they are replaced by red berries.

Found widely across North America.

Star-flowered Solomon's Seal   *Smilacina stellata*

Very similar to false Solomon's seal, star-flowered Solomon's seal grows only 1 to 2 feet tall and has fewer flowers at the tip of the stems. Its flowers are cream-colored or white; the berries are bright red. It, too, grows in shady woodlands.

Found across northern North America, south along the Pacific coast from British Columbia to California, and in the Rocky Mountains.

False Lily-of-the-valley
Maianthemum dilatatum

Star-flowered Solomon's Seal
Smilacina stellata

False Solomon's Seal
Smilacina racemosa

Star-flowered Solomon's Seal
Smilacina stellata

Wood Trillium   *Trillium ovatum*

Wood trillium is one of the Northwest's favorite wildflowers. Beginning to bloom in late March, when much of the rest of the forest floor is still clothed in winter brown, the large white blossoms stand out against the subdued background. Growing from 6 to 24 inches tall, each trillium bears three whorled leaves near the upper portion of the stem. These leaves cradle the three-petaled flower, which has its own short stalk. As the flower matures, its pure white color turns pale pink, and finally, deep rose.

Trilliums are among the most familiar of North American wildflowers. Because they bloom so early and are so beautiful, they often find their way into springtime bouquets. A word of caution is appropriate here. A great amount of stored food stuff from the previous year is expended to produce the flowering stem. The trillium has only three leaves with which to manufacture new food for growth. The picking of the flowering stem usually results in the death of the entire plant. Without the green leaves and stem, the plant cannot survive. So . . . leave the flowers in the field to enjoy next year.

Found from British Columbia to central California, east to Colorado and Wyoming.

Similar Plant: **Sessile trillium** (*Trillium angustipetulum*) is easily distinguished from the wood trillium because its flower is nestled against the three leaves. Lacking a stalk of its own, the flower is sessile. The three petals are a deep red or maroon color, and the leaves are mottled with shades of green. This species is common in the shady borders of redwood groves. Look for it in Prairie Creek Redwoods State Park.

Found in northern California and into southwestern Oregon.

Wood Trillium   *Trillium ovatum*

Sessile Trillium   *Trillium angustipetulum*

ORCHID FAMILY Orchidaceae

Orchids growing in wetlands are described on page 52.

Calypso *Calypso bulbosa*

This delicate member of the large orchid family is one of the most beautiful of our native orchids. That it is beloved by many people is attested to by the large number of common names that have been fondly bestowed on it: fairy slipper, deer-head orchid, Venus slipper, slipper orchid, angel slipper, redwoods orchid. The distinctive slipper-shaped flower rides atop a short, 6-inch-tall stalk, which has a sheathing, scalelike round leaf at its base. The flower is a reddish purple color and appears in May. After the flower withers, the single leaf also wilts, making the entire plant nearly undetectable during most of the summer. In the fall, a new leaf emerges from the small corm (the underground bulblike swelling at the base of the stem). This leaf then persists throughout the winter months.

The genus name *Calypso* is derived from the Greek, meaning "hidden" or "covered from view." Indeed, this little plant is well named, for it thrives only when growing in the deep duff of moist woodlands, where its diminutive size makes it easy to overlook.

Found throughout much of western and northern North America, and also in northern Europe and Asia.

POPPY FAMILY Papaveraceae

A poppy found along coastal bluffs and fields is described on page 96.

Corydalis *Corydalis scouleri*

Corydalis is closely related to the more familiar bleedingheart (see below). Its flowers are composed of four pink petals, arranged in pairs. One of the outer petals is spurred or sack-shaped. The resulting flower is a long, tubular affair, about a half inch long. The spur is twice as long as the rest of the petal. The rose-colored flowers are clustered at the end of a 10- to 20-inch-tall leafy stem. The seeds are encased in a fat, cylindrical capsule that explodes at the slightest touch, catapulting the seeds a considerable distance.

Found from British Columbia to Oregon.

Wild Bleedingheart *Dicentra formosa*

Bleedingheart flowers are uniquely heart-shaped baskets composed of four pale purple or pink petals. Slightly less than an inch long, they hang from 10- to 20-inch-tall stems. Bleedingheart leaves rise from stout rootstocks and are finely divided, somewhat resembling a fern leaf. You'll find these flowers in full bloom in the springtime and the early part of the summer; a few blossoms may still be found in sheltered places in July or August. Bleedingheart grows best in moist, shady woodlands, amid the moss of redwoods, Douglas fir, spruce, and hemlock.

Found from British Columbia south through western California.

Calypso *Calypso bulbosa*   **Corydalis** *Corydalis scouleri*

Wild Bleedingheart *Dicentra formosa*   **Wild Bleedingheart** *Dicentra formosa*

PURSLANE FAMILY   Portulacaceae

A member of the purslane family found along coastal bluffs and meadows is described on page 98.

Miner's Lettuce   *Claytonia perfoliata*

Miner's lettuce sprawls across the forest duff in dry woodlands or hugs the ground in a tight rosette of basal leaves in sandy openings, especially in dune areas that are partially vegetated or moist in the spring. It inhabits a variety of places from the coast and valley bottoms to forested mountains. It is easily distinguished from the closely related candyflower by the two leaves on the floral stem that completely enclose it, while those on candyflower are separate.

The name miner's lettuce comes from the plant's edible leaves. It is common in the mountain foothills that were frequented by pioneer prospectors. These miners probably learned of the plant from Native Americans. Early accounts relate how Indians gathered the plant or simply ate it in place. The succulent leaves can be eaten either cooked or raw, like any other green. Mixed with other raw vegetables, it makes an excellent salad.

Found throughout most of the western states.

Candyflower   *Claytonia sibirica*

Although the individual flowers are small, candyflower, also called western spring beauty, often sprawls over the ground in dense shade, dotting the forest floor with its white flowers. Look carefully at these five-petaled flowers: each petal has a notch in the tip. Most of the leaves are basal, meaning they emerge from the base of the plant on their own stems. The 5- to 12-inch flowering stem, however, also has two leaves. These are sessile, meaning they have no petiole, but are attached directly to the flowering stem and do not have a stalk of their own.

Candyflower often carpets the open forest floor beneath sitka spruce and shore pine with a mat of white blossoms in early spring.

Found throughout most of the western states.

Miner's Lettuce   *Claytonia perfoliata*

Candyflower   *Claytonia sibirica*

SAXIFRAGE FAMILY Saxifragaceae

Fringecup *Tellima grandifolia*

Fringecup is well named. Each flower is a small, cup-shaped affair with fringed edges that turn backward. Arranged linearly along a stem from 1 to 3 feet tall, the flowers vary in color from pink or red to pale green or white. Most of the leaves are basal. Fringecups can be found growing in shaded spots among the mossy rocks and boulders that form most of the high basalt cliffs of the coast. They bloom in April, May, and June. They also grow inland in moist, shaded woodlands.

Found from southern Alaska to central California.

Youth-on-age *Tolmiea menziesii*

Also called pig-a-back and thousand mothers, the most interesting characteristic of youth-on-age does not occur until late summer or fall. The 1- to 3-inch-wide leaves are heart-shaped, with irregularly lobed margins. The plant can reproduce small buds at the base of these leaves, thereby making each leaf appear to carry a second, smaller leaf, giving rise to the plant's common names. Many people collect youth-on-age to use for a houseplant because of its rich, leafy growth. The flowers, which are maroon or even rust colored, occur on a linear stem 1 to 2 feet long and bloom in May and June.

The scientific name honors two great men of the early Northwest. Dr. William F. Tolmie was a surgeon at Fort Vancouver for the Hudson's Bay Company during the mid-1800s. Archibald Menzies was a naturalist with the 1790–1795 Vancouver Expedition, which explored the Pacific coast. His observations added greatly to our early knowledge of the Northwest.

Found from Alaska south through California.

SUNFLOWER FAMILY Compositae

Other members of the sunflower family are described on pages 26 to 30, 62, 102 to 110, and 140.

Coltsfoot *Petasites frigidus*

Competing with skunk cabbage for the title of "earliest blooming wildflower," coltsfoot begins to emerge from the soil in mid-February and March. First a miniature parasol-shaped leaf unfolds, then the buttonlike flower appears on its stalk. When it first begins to bloom, the flowering stalk is merely a few inches tall; however, after a few weeks it grows to about 12 inches. The round cluster of flowers is at the tip of a thick stem that has scalelike leaves along its length. The tubular florets of the flower heads are pale pink or lavender, sometimes white. As they wither, the broad leaf expands and remains for the rest of the summer. These leaves have soft, woolly hairs on their undersides and grow nearly a foot across. Coltsfoot may be found in the leaf duff of lowland forests and along shady, moist roadbanks.

Found across northern North America and south through the Pacific states to central California. Also found in northern Europe and Asia.

Fringecup *Tellima grandifolia*

Youth-on-age *Tolmiea menziesii* **Coltsfoot** *Petasites frigidus*

VIOLET FAMILY

Violaceae

The violet family is mainly valued for its flowers. The well-loved garden pansies and violets are familiar to many. The family has 200 species, which are found in nearly all climates. Through hybridization, many additional varieties have been produced.

Most of us think of violets as purple flowers; however, most of the Northwest's native violets are yellow or a combination of white, blue, or yellow. A purple-flowered violet found on grassy headlands is described on page 110.

The irregular five-petaled flowers have a distinctive shape. There are two lateral petals, two upper petals, and one lower petal that is spurred at the base.

The *Viola* genus has an interesting backup mechanism for propagating. The large showy flowers are often not fertile and do not produce an abundant supply of seeds. But later in the season, small flowers bloom near the ground, which do not open and are self-fertilized. Thus, a supplemental seed source helps insure the continuity of the species.

Wood Violet

Viola glabella

This yellow-flowered violet has erect, leafy stems 6 to 12 inches tall and broad, heart-shaped leaves. They spread from a horizontal rootstock, a trait that makes it a good ground cover for native gardens. The irregular five-petaled flower has the characteristic violet shape; in wood violet, the lateral and lower petals are dark-veined.

Found from Alaska through California.

Evergreen Violet

Viola sempervirens

Common in coastal woodlands, especially in the deep duff of redwood forests, this yellow-flowered violet, also called redwoods violet, has prostrate stems and round, evergreen leaves. The lower and lateral petals are marked with purple.

Found from British Columbia to California.

Wood Violet *Viola glabella*

Evergreen Violet *Viola sempervirens*

WOOD SORREL FAMILY   Oxalidaceae

Redwood Sorrel   *Oxalis oregana*

Also called wood sorrel, the dainty, clover-shaped leaves of this ground-hugging plant often cover much of the forest floor at lower elevations. They fold together at night and on cloudy days and droop when exposed to strong sunlight. When massed together, the overall effect is of a dense, leafy carpet that is often more noticeable than the flowers, which are tucked down between the leaves. There is quite a bit of variation in the color of the flowers. Under the redwoods they often exhibit a deep pink color, while farther north along the coast they are usually white. There may also be a difference in the leaves; some have distinctive white markings, while others are a uniform green.

The genus name *Oxalis* refers to the oxalic acid found in the plant, which gives the edible leaves a rather tart taste. The leaves add a pleasing tang to green salads. Wood sorrel is sometimes introduced into shaded gardens as a ground cover. A fairly aggressive plant, it spreads rapidly by underground stems. These allow it to quickly fill in a shady nook, often to the exclusion of other small plants.

Found from the Olympic Peninsula to northern California.

Redwood Sorrel   *Oxalis oregana*

Wildflower Photography

All of the photos in this book were made with a 35mm single-lens reflex (SLR) camera. The wildflowers were mostly photographed in their natural setting, using available light. While there are advantages to using artificial lighting, the natural lighting helps depict the conditions where the plant grows and hints at the type of place where additional plants may be found. Equipment need not be extensive; a good camera, a close-up lens or attachment, a light meter, and a tripod are the only essentials. Remember, though: It takes more than the proper equipment for a good photograph.

Good wildflower photos are not taken; they are created. The single most important factor is patience. Lots of it. You must take the time to make sure the photo you are about to create is the best you can possibly do. Just as important as tripping the shutter is an awareness of the right situation, the right flower, the right setting. Is the lighting adequate? Is the wind calm? Is the background uncluttered, clear of fence lines, power poles, or reflective material? Is the flower a good specimen, not half-eaten by insects or partially wilted? Are you in a creative mood and not in a hurry? If you can answer yes to these questions, you are ready to photograph. Be willing to take the time to search out the best possible situation before you set up your camera. The following suggestions will help you create your photo.

1. Don't be afraid to get as close as you can to the flower you wish to photograph. If the specimen is very small and will not fill the frame, find a clump or group of flowers that will. Don't waste a portion of your photograph unless the background really adds to the character and composition of the photo.

2. Look at the background and foreground through the lens. Will anything detract from your chosen subject matter? Is there a protruding stick or blade of grass? Is the background a confusion of sunlight and shadow that may give your light meter a false reading and produce a

crazy quilt background? Is sunlight bouncing off a shiny rock or blade of grass, potentially causing a glare that could ruin an otherwise good photo? A carefully placed rock can help remove an unwanted tuft of grass or a piece of string can tie back an unwanted branch. A large piece of dark brown or green blotter paper (poster paper usually has a shiny surface) placed behind a plant can separate a confusing background from your subject.

3. The coast is known for its windy weather. Even on a calm day, there is often a faint breeze. The best time to photograph is in the morning, when the wind is more apt to be calm. Slender plant stems tend to sway with the slightest wind. With a breeze, they will dance wildly. In that case, you should simply call it a day and return at another time. Even with a fast shutter speed, the photo is likely to be a blur. If the wind is intermittent, you may want to be patient and wait to snap your photo between gusts of wind.

4. When photographing a white or yellow flower in bright sunlight, take your light reading directly from the flower to avoid overexposing your photograph. The light reflected from the petals will provide a different reading than a reading that includes the darker background.

5. Bright sunlight will cast dark shadows on your subject, producing a distracting background. Avoid photographing at midday and aim for early morning or evening. Try to photograph on cloudy but bright days. These conditions soften shadows, resulting in a more pleasing photo.

6. It is essential to use a tripod when photographing in the faint light of dense forest. Many tripods, however, do not allow the camera to be placed on or near the ground. Small beanbags or similar items can be used to prop up your camera in the appropriate position for your photograph.

As you practice taking photos, you'll develop your own techniques for better photography. Keep in mind, though: Your camera cannot create a photo; only you can do that.

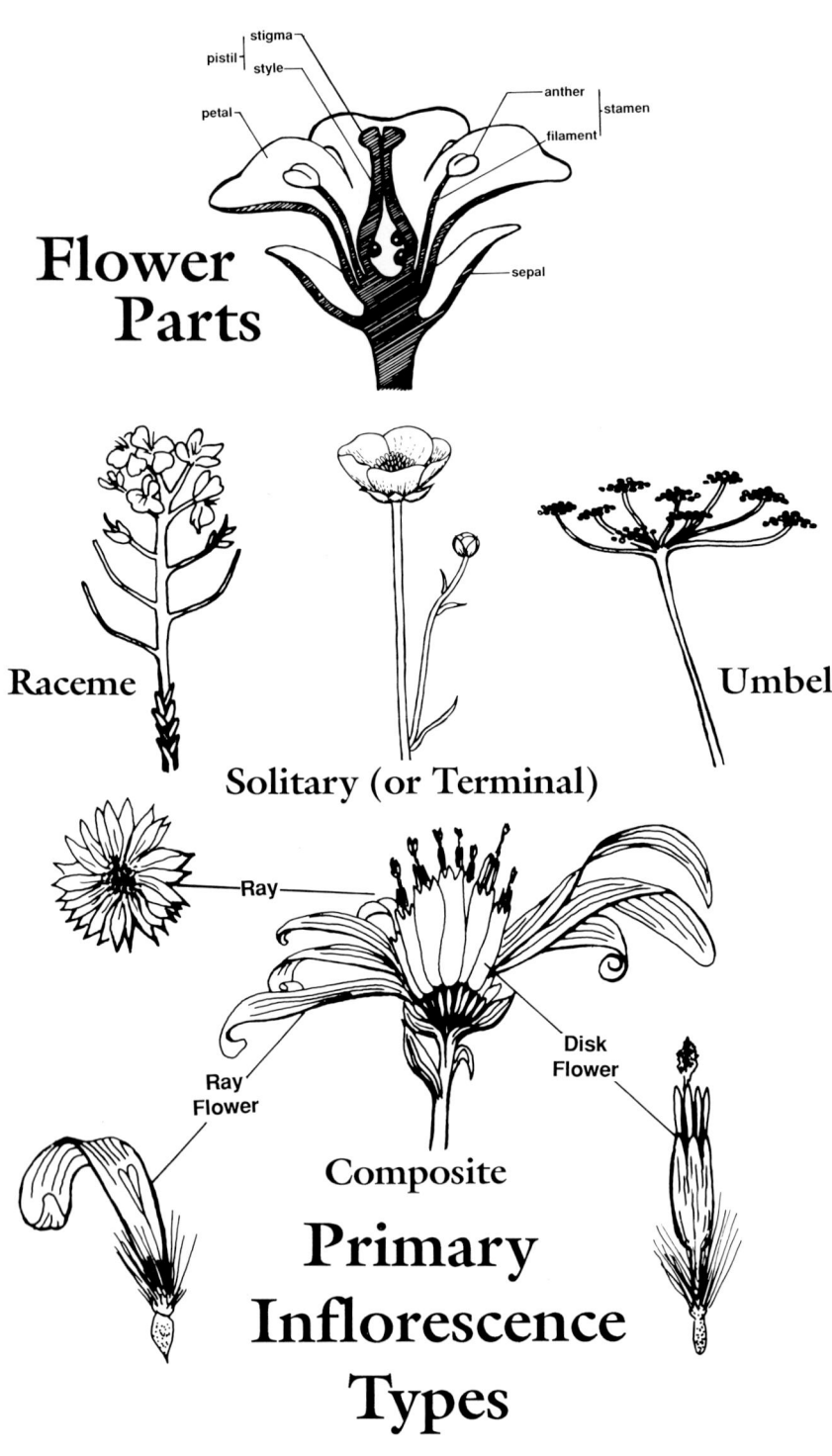

Flower Parts

pistil { stigma, style

petal

anther, filament } stamen

sepal

Raceme

Solitary (or Terminal)

Umbel

Ray

Ray Flower

Disk Flower

Composite

Primary Inflorescence Types

Leaf Shapes

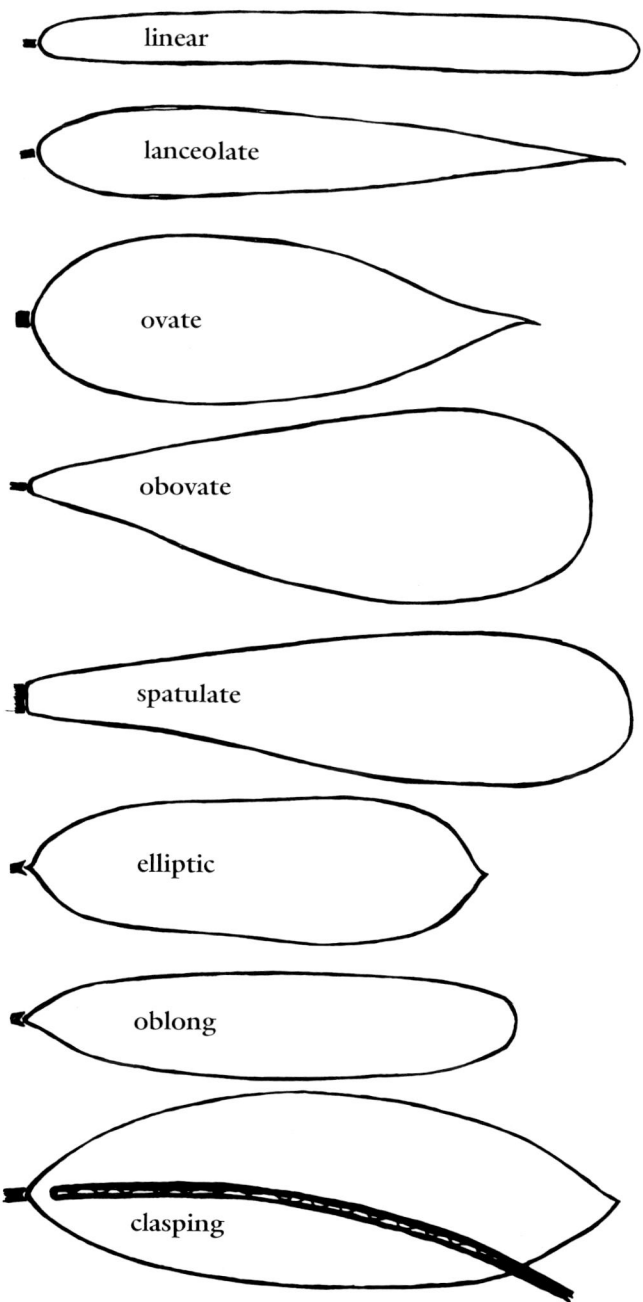

linear

lanceolate

ovate

obovate

spatulate

elliptic

oblong

clasping

Leaf Arrangements

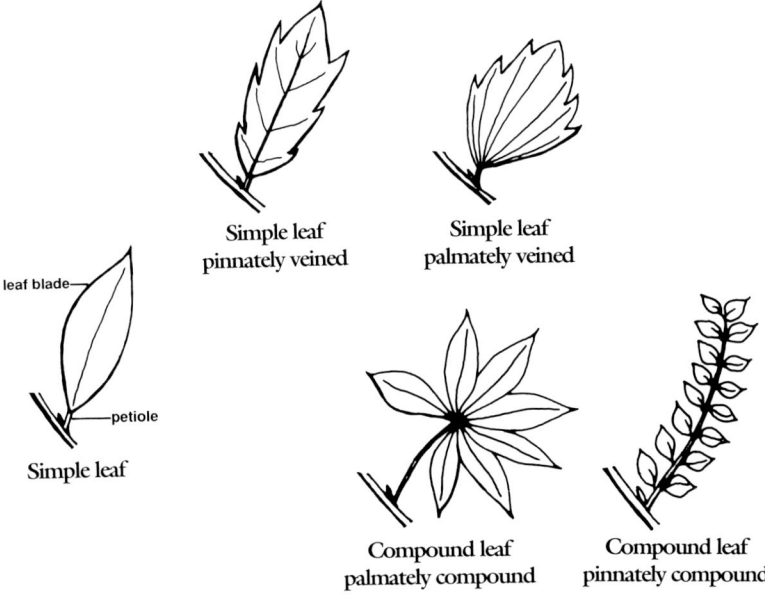

Simple leaf
pinnately veined

Simple leaf
palmately veined

leaf blade

petiole

Simple leaf

Compound leaf
palmately compound

Compound leaf
pinnately compound

Leaf Structure

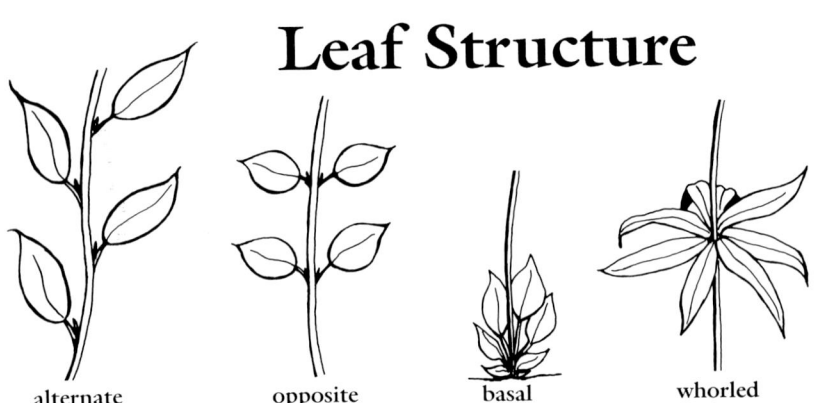

alternate

opposite

basal

whorled

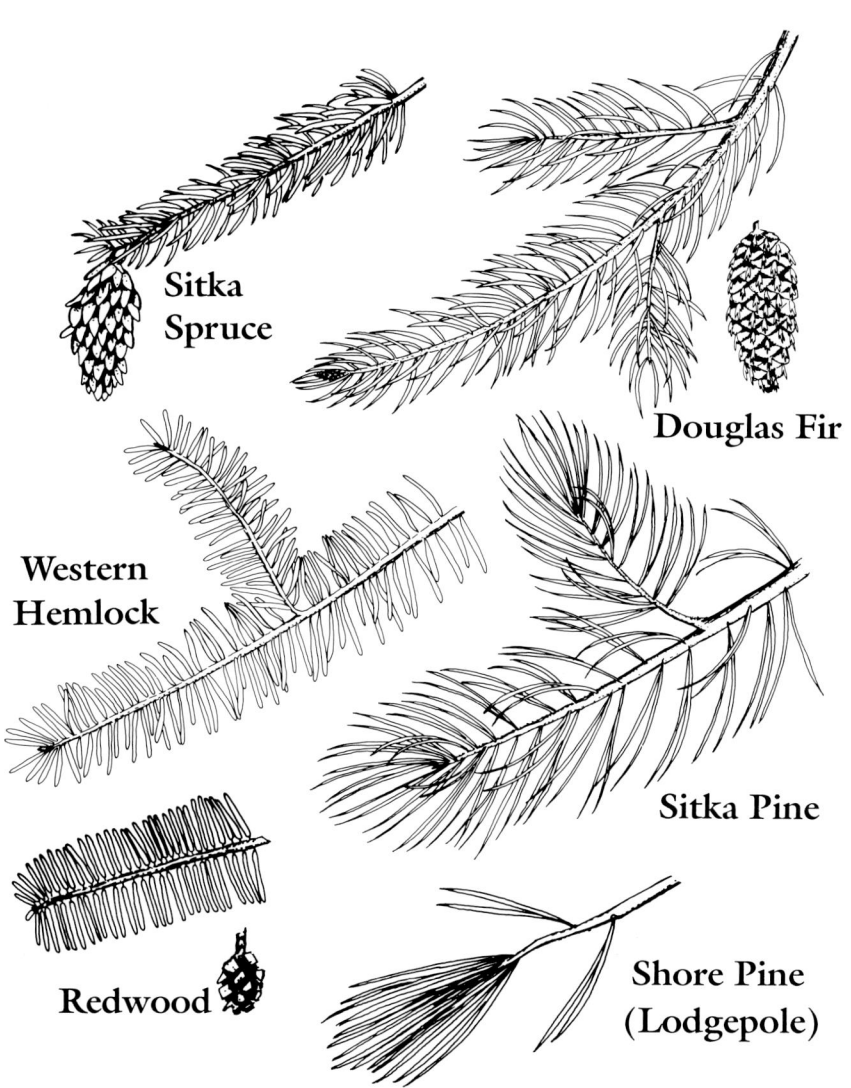

Sitka
Spruce

Douglas Fir

Western
Hemlock

Sitka Pine

Redwood

Shore Pine
(Lodgepole)

Coastal Forest Conifers

Glossary

Alternate. Usually referring to leaf arrangement, when there is only one leaf in a given location on a stem.

Annual. A plant that lives only one year.

Anther. The pollen-bearing part of the stamen.

Axillary. In the angle between a leaf and stem.

Basal. At the base.

Biennial. Requiring two growing seasons to complete a life cycle.

Blade. Expanded part; for instance, the blade of a leaf.

Bract. Modified or reduced leaf.

Bulb. Underground cluster of leaves for food storage.

Cleft. Cut or divided almost to the middle.

Compound. Divided into more than one part, as opposed to simple (as in leaf).

Corm. Bulblike, fleshy portion of a stem, usually underground, used for food storage.

Corolla. Inner circle of flower parts (petals).

Deciduous. Falling off at the end of the growing season.

Decumbent. Lying on the ground near the base, but with the tip elevated.

Decurrent. Base of leaf with small wings that partially clasp the stem.

Deflation plain. Flat, sandy plain where wind has removed the sand down to the water table.

Disk flower. The tubular flower in members of the sunflower family, such as the yellow flowers in the center of a daisy.

Dissected. Deeply cut or divided into many parts.

Elliptic. Elliptical (flattened circle) leaf form.

Entire. Not toothed or cut.

Evergreen. Lasting year-round, throughout the year.

Exotic. Not of local origin.

Filament. The threadlike stalk of a stamen.

Foredune. First ridge of sand paralleling the beach.

Gland. Organ that secretes material.

Habitat. Place where a plant grows.

Head. Very compact cluster of flowers, usually at the tip of a stem.

Herb. Plant without woody parts.

Lanceolate. Lance-shaped leaf form; narrowly elongate, tapering to a pointed tip.

Lateral. At the side.

Leaflet. One of the parts of a compound leaf.

Linear. Leaf form with nearly parallel sides, narrower than oblong.

Lip. One of the parts of a two-lipped corolla.

Lobe. Shallow division on a leaf.

Node. Place on a stem that bears a leaf.

Oblong. Leaf form in which the length is much greater than the width and the edges are parallel for most of their length.

Obovate. Leaf form shaped with the narrowest part at the base and the widest at the tip.

Opposite. Usually referring to leaf arrangement, when two leaves occur directly opposite each other on a stem.

Ovate. Leaf form shaped with the broadest part at the base.

Palmate. Spreading like the fingers of a palm (as compared to pinnate); usually referring to the arrangement of leaflets of a compound leaf.

Panicle. Branching flower cluster.

Pedicel. Stalk or stem of a single flower.

Pendant. Hanging.

Perennial. Plant lasting from one year to the next.

Petal. One of the floral parts, usually colored.

Petiole. Leaf stalk.

Pinnate. Arranged along the side of a central stalk (as compared to palmate); usually referring to the arrangement of leaflets of a compound leaf.

Pistil. Central, seed-bearing organ of a flower.

Prickle. Thornlike projection.

Prostrate. Growing flat on the ground.

Pubescent. Hairy.

Raceme. Flower cluster in which the individual flower pedicels are distributed linearly along a central stalk and the lower flowers open first.

Ray flower. Flat, elongate flowers of a composite floral head of the sunflower family, such as the white marginal flowers of a daisy.

Rhizome. Underground stem.

Rootstock. Underground rootlike stem.

Rosette. Collection of leaves arranged circularly around the base of a plant.

Scorpioid. Coiled, curved.

Sepal. Parts of a flower below the petal, usually green.

Sessile. Stemless.

Sheath. The basal part of a leaf that encloses part of the stem.

Simple. One piece, as opposed to compound (in leaves).

Spathe. A large leaflike bract that encloses a cluster of flowers.

Spatulate. Narrow at the base and wider at the tip.

Spur. Saclike or tubular projection from either a sepal or a petal.

Stamen. Floral organ bearing the pollen.

Sterile. Not fertile; will not produce any seeds.

Stigma. Pollen-receiving part of the pistil.

Stolon. A runner or "sucker" that will root and form a new plant.

Style. Stemlike part of the pistil.

Succulent. Fleshy.

Taproot. Main descending root.

Tendril. Slender coiling stem or modified leaf used by a climbing plant to support itself.

Umbel. A flat-topped cluster of flowers in which the pedicels all seem to arise from the same level.

Vegetative. Reproducing by means other than seeds.

Whorl. Three or more similar organs radiating from the same spot, such as whorled leaves.

Selected References

Abrams, Leroy. *Illustrated Flora of the Pacific States*. Stanford: Stanford University Press, 1940, 1950, 1951, 1960. 4 volumes.

Ball, Edward K. *Early Uses of California Plants*. Berkeley: University of California Press, 1972.

Gunther, Erna. *Ethnobotany of Western Washington*. Seattle: University of Washington Press, 1973.

Hitchcock, C. L., A. Cronquist, M. Ownbey, and J. W. Thompson. *Vascular Plants of the Pacific Northwest*. Seattle: University of Washington Press, 1955, 1959, 1961, 1964. 5 volumes.

Hitchcock, C. Leo, and Arthur Cronquist. *Flora of the Pacific Northwest*. Seattle: University of Washington Press, 1973.

Hickman, James C., ed. *The Jepson Manual: Higher Plants of California*. Berkeley, Los Angeles, and London: University of California Press, 1993.

Munz, Philip A., and David D. Keck. *A California Flora and Supplement*. Berkeley: University of California Press, 1973.

Index

(Boldface numbers indicate pages with photographs.)

Abronia latifolia, 14, **15**
   umbellata, 14, **15**
Achillea millefolium, 102, **103**
Aizoaceae, 10
Ambrosia chamissonis, 26, **27**
American carrot, 90, **91**
Anagallis arvensis, 96, **97**
Anaphalis margaritacea, 102, **103**
Angelica, 88, **89**
Angelica hendersonii, 88, **89**
   lucida, 88
Aquilegia formosa, 70, **71**
Araceae, 36
Arbutus menziesii, 116, **117**
Arctostaphylos columbiana, 118, **119**
   uva-ursi, 118, **119**
Aristolochiaceae, 144
Armeria maritima, 80, **81**
Artemisia pycnocephala, 26, **27**
Arum family, 36
Aruncus dioicus, 132, **133**
Asarum caudatum, 144, **145**
Aster, beach, 26, **27**
   California, 104, **105**
Aster chilensis, 104, **105**
Azalea, western, 122, **123**

Baccharis pilularis, 140, **141**
Barberry family, 68
Beach gumweed, 28, **29**
Beach knotweed, 10, **11**
Beach morning glory, 16, **17**
Beach pea, 18, **19**
Beach primrose, 12, **13**
Beach sagewort, 26, **27**
Beach silvertop, 16, **17**

Beach silverweed, 26, **27**
Beach strawberry, 24, **25**
Bearberry, 118, **119**
Bearberry honeysuckle, 46, **47**
Bearbrush, 140
Beeplant, 42, **43**
Bellis perennis, 104, **105**
Berberidaceae, 68
Berberis acquifolium, 68, **69**
   nervosa, 68, **69**
Bird's foot trefoil, 54, **55**
Birthwort family, 144
Blackberry, Himalayan, 136, **137**
Blue blossom, 114, **115**
Blue dicks, 82
Blue gilia, 94, **95**
Blue-eyed grass, 80, **81**
Bluff mallow, 84, **85**
Bog orchid, slender, 52, **53**
Boschniakia hookeri, 144, **145**
   strobilacea, 144
Bramble, evergreen, 136
Brass buttons, 62, **63**
Broad-leaved stonecrop, 100, **101**
Brodiaea capitata, 82
   coronaria, 82, **83**
Brodiaea, harvest, 82, **83**
Broom-rape family, 144
Buckthorn family, 68, 114
Buckwheat family, 10
Burnet, 58, **59**
Bush honeysuckle, 46, **47**
Buttercup family, 38, 70-72
Buttercup, California, 72, **73**

174

creeping, 38, **39**
field, 72, **73**
small creeping, 38, **39**

Cakile edentula, 16, **17**
  maritima, 16, **17**
Calandrinia ciliata, 98, **99**
California aster, 104, **105**
California poppy, 96, **97**
Calypso, 154, **155**
Calypso bulbosa, 154, **155**
Calystegia soldanella, 16, **17**
Camas, common, 48, **49**
  Leichtlin's, 48, **49**
Camassia leichtlinii, 48, **49**
  quamash, 48, **49**
Camissonia cheiranthifolia, 12, **13**
Candyflower, 156, **157**
Caprifoliaceae, 46, 126
Carpetweed family, 10
Carpobrotus chilensis, 10, **11**
  edule, 10, **11**
Carrot, American, 90
  wild, 90, **91**
Caryophyllaceae, 22, 94
Castilleja ambigua, 42, **43**
  affinis, 74, **75**
  latifolia, 74, **75**
Cat's ear, 28, **29**
Cattail, broad-leaved, 40, **41**
Cattail family, 40
Ceanothus gloriosus, 68, **69**
  thysiflorus, 114, **115**
Centaurium erythraea, 44, **45**
Centaury, 44, **45**
Cerastium arvense, 94, **95**
Chaparral broom, 140, **141**
Checkerbloom, 84, **85**
Chenopodiaceae, 44
Chickweed, field, 94, **95**
Cicuta douglasii, 54
Cirsium vulgare, 104, **105**
Clarkia, 72, **73**
Clarkia amoena, 12, **13**
  unguiculata, 72, **73**
Claytonia perfoliata, 156, **157**
  sibirica, 156, **157**
Clintonia andrewsiana, 148, **149**
Clintonia, red, 148, **149**
Clover, marsh, 54, **55**

Coast buckwheat, 10, **11**
Coast paintbrush, 74, **75**
Coast strawberry, 24, **25**
Cobra lily, 56, **57**
Coltsfoot, 158, **159**
Columbine, 70, **71**
Common camas, 48, **49**
Common daisy, 108, **109**
Common thistle, 104, **105**
Compositae, 26-30, 62, 102-110,
  140, 158
Composite family, 26-30, 62, 102-
  110, 140, 158
Conium maculatum, 54, **55**
Convolvulaceae, 16
Corethrogyne californica, 26, **27**
Corydalis, 154, **155**
Corydalis scouleri, 154, **155**
Cotula coronopifolia, 62, **63**
Cow parsnip, 90, **91**
Coyote bush, 140, **141**
Crassulaceae, 100
Creeping buttercup, 38, **39**
Cruciferae, 16, 86
Cucumber, wild, 78, **79**
Cucuribitaceae, 78
Currant family, 114
Currant, pink-flowering, 114, **115**
Cytisus scoparius, 130, **131**

Daisy, common, 108, **109**
Daisy, seaside, 106, **107**
Darlingtonia californica, 56, **57**
Daucus carota, 90, **91**
  pusillus, 90
Delphinium menziesii, 70, **71**
Dicentra formosa, 154, **155**
Digitalis purpurea, 74, **75**
Disporum hookeri, 148
  smithii, 148, **149**
Douglas spirea, 58, **59**
Drosera rotundifolia, 60, **61**
Droseraceae, 60
Dudleya farinosa, 100, **101**

Elderberry, 126, **127**
  blue, 126, **127**
English daisy, 104, **105**
Epilobium angustifolium, 116, **117**
Epipactis gigantea, 52, **53**

Ericaceae, 46, 116-124
Erigeron glaucus, 106, **107**
Eriogonum latifolium, 10, **11**
Eriophyllum lanatum, 106, **107**
    staechadifolium, 140, **141**
Erysimum capitatum, 86, **87**
Eschscholtzia californica, 96, **97**
Evening primrose, 12, **13**
Evening primrose family, 12, 72, 116
Evergreen bramble, 136

Fairy bells, 148
Fairy lanterns, 148, **149**
Fairy slipper, 154, **155**
False lily-of-the-valley, 150, **151**
False Solomon's seal, 150, **151**
Farewell-to-spring, 12. **13**
Figwort, 42, **43**
Figwort family, 42, 74-76, 146
Fireweed, 116, **117**
Flax family, 76
Flax, wild, 76, **77**
Footsteps-of-spring, 92, **93**
Four o'clock family, 14
Foxglove, 74, **75**
Fragaria chiloensis, 24, **25**
French broom, 130, **131**
Fringecup, 158, **159**
Fritillaria affinis, 82, **83**

Garrya elliptica, 140, **141**
    fremontii, 140
Garryaceae, 140
Gaultheria shallon, 120, **121**
Gentian, common, 44, **45**
Gentian family, 44
Gentiana sceptrum, 44, **45**
Gentianaceae, 44
Genista monospessulanus, 130, **131**
Gilia capitata, 94, **95**
Ginger, wild, 144, **145**
Glaux maritima, 56, **57**
Glehnia littoralis, 16, **17**
Goat's beard, 132, **133**
Gold fields, 106, **107**
Golden-eyed grass, 48, **49**
Goldenrod, Canada, 110, **111**
    dune, 28, **29**
Gooseberry, prickly, 114
Goosefoot family, 44

Gorse, 130, **131**
Gourd family, 78
Grass, blue-eyed, 80, **81**
    golden-eyed, 48, **49**
Grindelia integrifolia, 62, **63**
    stricta, 28, **29**
Grossulariaceae, 114
Ground cone, 144, **145**
    California, 144
Grouse flower, 146, **147**
Gumweed, 62, **63**
    beach, 28, **29**

Hawkbit, 28
Heath family, 46, 116-124
Hen-and-chickens, 100, **101**
Heracleum lanatum, 90, **91**
Hollyhock, wild, 84, **85**
Holodiscus discolor, 98, **99**
Honeysuckle family, 46, 126
Honkenya peploides, 22, **23**
Hottentot fig, 10, **11**
Huckleberry, evergreen, 124, **125**
    red, 124, **125**
Hydrophyllaceae, 30
Hypericaceae, 60
Hypericum anagalloides, 60, **61**
Hypochaeris radicata, 28, **29**

Indian plum, 134, **135**
Ink-berry, 46
Iridaceae, 48, 80
Iris douglasiana, 80, **81**
    tenax, 80, **81**
Iris family, 48, 80
Iris, wild, 80, **81**

Jaumea, 62, **63**
Jaumea carnosa, 62, **63**

Kalmia polifolia, 46, **47**
Kinnikinnick, 118, **119**

Labiatae, 50, 86
Labrador tea, 46, **47**
Ladies' tresses, 52, **53**
Larkspur, field, 70, **71**
Lasthenia macrantha, 106, **107**
Lathyrus japonicus, 18, **19**
    littoralis, 18, **19**
Layia platyglossa, 108, **109**

Leadwort family, 80
Ledum glandulosum, 46, **47**
Leguminosae, 18-21, 54, 130
Leontodon nudicaulis, 28
Leucanthemum vulgare, 108, **109**
Liliaceae, 48, 82, 128, 148-152
Lilium columbianum, 128, **129**
Lily family, 48, 82, 128, 148-152
Lily, tiger, 128, **129**
Linaceae, 76
Linum bienne, 76, **77**
Live-forever, 100, **101**
Lizard tail, 140, **141**
Lomatium utriculatum, 92, **93**
Lonicera involucrata, 46, **47**
Lotus corniculatus, 54, **55**
Lupine, bush, 20, **21**
    seashore, 20, **21**
Lupinus arboreus, 20, **21**
    littoralis, 20, **21**
Lysichitum americanum, 36, **37**

Madrone, 116, **117**
Maianthemum dilatatum, 150, **151**
Mallow, bluff, 84, **85**
Mallow family, 84
Malvaceae, 84
Manzanita, hairy, 118, **119**
Marah oreganus, 78, **79**
Marsh clover, 54, **55**
Mentha arvensis, 50, **51**
Milkwort, sea, 56, **57**
Mimulus aurantiacus, 76, **77**
    dentatus, 42
    guttatus, 42, **43**
Miner's lettuce, 156, **157**
Mint family, 50, 86
Mint, wild, 50, **51**
Mission bells, 82, **83**
Monkeyflower, bush, 76, **77**
    coast, 42
    common, 42, **43**
Morning glory family, 16
Mustard family, 16, 86
Myrica californica, 64, **65**
Myricaceae, 64

Nuphar luteum, 64, **65**
Nyctaginaceae, 14
Nymphacaceae, 64

Ocean spray, 98, **99**
Oemleria cerasiformis, 134, **135**
Oenanthe sarmentosa, 54, **55**
Oenothera hookeri, 12, **13**
Onagraceae, 12, 72, 116
Orchid family, 52, 154
Orchidaceae, 52, 154
Oregon grape, 68, **69**
Oregon stonecrop, 100, **101**
Orobanchaceae, 144
Owl clover, 42, **43**
Oxalidaceae, 162
Oxalis oregana, 162, **163**

Paintbrush, coast, 74, **75**
    seaside, 76, **77**
Papaveraceae, 96, 154
Parentucellia, 76, 77
Parentucellia viscosa, 76, **77**
Parsley family, 16, 54, 88-92
Pea family, 18-21, 54, 130
Pearly everlasting, 102, **103**
Petasites frigidus, 158, **159**
Phacelia argentea, 30, **31**
Phlox family, 94
Pickleweed, 44, **45**
Pimpernel, 96, **97**
Pink family, 22, 94
Pink-flowering currant, 114, **115**
Pitcher plant family, 56
Plantaginaceae, 22
Plantago maritima, 22, **23**
Plantain family, 22
Plantain, seaside, 22, **23**
Platanthera stricta, 52, **53**
Plum, Indian, 134, **135**
Plumbaginaceae, 80
Point Reyes creeper, 68, **69**
Poison hemlock, 54, **55**
Polemoniaceae, 94
Polygonaceae, 10
Polygonum paronychia, 10, **11**
Pond lily, 64, **65**
Poppy, California, 96, **97**
Poppy family, 96, 154
Portulaceae, 98, 156
Potentilla anserina, 24, **25**
Primrose family, 56, 96
Primulaceae, 56, 96
Prunella vulgaris, 86, **87**

Purslane family, 98, 156

Ragwort, tansy, 108, **109**
Ranunculaceae, 38, 70-72
Ranunculus californicus, 72, **73**
    flammula, 38, **39**
    occidentalis, 72, **73**
    repens, 38, **39**
Raphanus sativus, 86, **87**
Red clintonia, 148, **149**
Red maids, 98, **99**
Redwood sorrel, 162, **163**
Redwoods orchid, 154, **155**
Rhamnaceae, 68, 114
Rhododendron macrophyllum, 122, **123**
    occidentale, 122, **123**
Rhododendron, Pacific, 122, **123**
Ribes menziesii, 114
    sanguineum, 114, **115**
Rosa nutkana, 134, **135**
Rosaceae, 24, 58, 98, 132-138
Rose family, 24, 58, 98, 132-138
Rose, wild, 134, **135**
Rubus discolor, 136, **137**
    laciniatus, 136
    parviflorus, 138, **139**
    spectablis, 138, **139**

Salal, 120, **121**
Salicornia virginica, 44, **45**
Salmonberry, 138, **139**
Sambucus cerulea, 126, **127**
    racemosa, 126, **127**
Sand verbena, pink, 14, **15**
Sand verbena, yellow, 14, **15**
Sanguisorba officianalis, 58, **59**
Sanicula arctopoides, 92, **93**
Sarraceniaceae, 56
Saxifragaceae, 158
Saxifrage family, 158
Scotch broom, 130, **131**
Scrophularia californica, 42, **43**
Scrophulariaceae, 42, 74-76, 146
Sea fig, 10, **11**
Sea milkwort, 56, **57**
Sea purslane, 22, **23**
Seabeach sandwort, 22, **23**
Searocket, 16, **17**
Seaside daisy, 106, **107**

Seaside paintbrush, 74, **75**
Seaside tansy, 30, **31**
Seaside woolly sunflower, 140, **141**
Sedum oreganum, 100, **101**
    spatulifolium, 100, **101**
Self-heal, 86, **87**
Senecio jacobaea, 108, **109**
Sidalcea hirtipes, 84, **85**
    malavaeflora, 84, **85**
Silk tassel, 140, **141**
Silk tassel family, 140
Silky beach pea, 18, **19**
Silverweed, beach, 26, **27**
    Pacific, 24, **25**
Silvery phacelia, 30, **31**
Sisyrinchium bellum, 80, **81**
    californicum, 48, **49**
Skunk cabbage, 36, **37**
Smilacina racemosa, 150, **151**
    stellata, 150, **151**
Snake-root, 92, **93**
Snow queen, 146, **147**
Solidago canadensis, 110, **111**
    spathulata, 28, **29**
Solomon's seal, false, 150, **151**
    star-flowered, 150, **151**
Sorrel, redwood, 162, **163**
    wood, 162, **163**
Spiraea douglasii, 58, **59**
Spiranthes romanzoffiana, 52, **53**
Spring gold, 92, **93**
Spring queen, 146, **147**
St. John's wort family, 60
Star-flowered Solomon's seal, 150, **151**
Stonecrop family, 100
Stonecrop, broad-leaved, 100, **101**
    Oregon, 100, **101**
Strawberry, beach, 24, **25**
Stream orchis, 52, **53**
Sundew, 60, **61**
Sundew family, 60
Sunflower family, 26-30, 62, 102-110, 140, 158
Sunflower, seaside woolly, 140, **141**
Sunflower, woolly, 106, **107**
Swamp laurel, 46, **47**
Sweet gale family, 64
Sweet pea, 18
Synthyris reniformis, 146, **147**

Tanacetum camporatum, 30, **31**
Tansy ragwort, 108, **109**
Tansy, seaside, 30, **31**
Tansy, western, 30
Taraxacum officinale, 28
Tellima grandifolia, 158, **159**
Thimbleberry, 138, **139**
Thistle, common, 104, **105**
Thrift, 80, **81**
Tidy tips, 108, **109**
Tiger lily, 128, **129**
Tinker's penny, 60, **61**
Tolmiea menziesii, 158, **159**
Trifolium wormskioldii, 54, **55**
Trillium angustipetulum, 152, **153**
    ovatum, 152, **153**
Trillium, sessile, 152, **153**
    wood, 152, **153**
Twinberry, 46
Typha latifolia, 40, **41**
Typhaceae, 40

Ulex europaea, 130, **131**
Umbelliferae, 16, 54, 88-92

Vaccinium ovatum, 124, **125**
    parvifolium, 124, **125**
Venus slipper, 154, **155**
Vetch, giant, 20, **21**
Vicia gigantea, 20, **21**
Viola adunca, 110, **111**

glabella, 160, **161**
sempervirens, 160, **161**
Violaceae, 110, 160
Violet, evergreen, 160, **161**
    western blue, 110, **111**
    wood, 160, **161**
Violet family, 110, 160

Wallflower, 86, **87**
Water hemlock, 54
Water lily family, 64
Water parsley, 54, **55**
Waterleaf family, 30
Wax myrtle, 64, **65**
Wild bleedingheart, 154, **155**
Wild carrot, 90, **91**
Wild cucumber, 78, **79**
Wild flax, 76, **77**
Wild ginger, 144, **145**
Wild hollyhock, 84, **85**
Wild iris, 80, **81**
Wild radish, 86, **87**
Wild rose, 134, **135**
Wood sorrel, 162, **163**
Wood sorrel family, 162

Yarrow, 102, **103**
    golden, 106, **107**, 140, **141**
Yellow-mats, 92, **93**
Yellow pond lily, 64, **65**
Youth-on-age 158, **159**